LOGA

The Life and Times of J.D. Logan… a Matjiesfontein Chronicle

by Robert N. Toms

Mallard Publishers

First Published 1997
Second Edition 1998
Limited Edition

Published by Mallard Publishers
P.O. Box 36012
Glosderry 7702
Claremont
South Africa

ISBN 1 875076 13 1

Edited by P.J. and C.A.L. Harpur (assisted by M. Wessels)
Cover picture depicting Matjiesfontein by courtesy of Tony Grogan

Printing by Wescape Easibind
Repro and Graphics by Citi Graphics
DTP by Kerryn Grogan

To Corinne

Acknowledgments

We should like to thank Major John Buist, David Rawdon and all those others who have given us such invaluable assistance with this book, without whom it could not have been such a success.

Introduction by David Rawdon

I feel very honoured to be asked to write the introduction to Bob Toms' book on James Logan, especially as I have never been asked to write an introduction before and never expected to be.

I thoroughly enjoyed reading Logan's Way, perhaps more so than the average person because of my close connection with Jimmy Logan through having owned the Village for the past 30 years. I have always greatly admired Logan and all he did at Matjiesfontein, marvelling at a man who was so much ahead of his time. It was indeed fortuitous that the Village was left in the Logan Trust so that consequently, no damage could be done it nor any alterations effected. When I took it over it was merely shabby - all was in a state of amazing preservation. Rather ironically, our greatest challenge consisted in making bathrooms for every room!

Reading Bob's book, which tells us so much of the man, one cannot help but be struck by what an amazing person he was, working himself up from virtually nothing to become a man of wealth, power and influence.

Before she married, my mother lived mainly in Cape Town and Stellenbosch. Just prior to the First World War she went to teach domestic science in Kimberley, where she met my father, an American dentist. After the war they married and settled in South Africa.

I remember so well as a child Mum telling us of the

long trips by train from Cape Town to Kimberly and of course, about the hot soup at Matjiesfontein!

The book itself of course tells of far more than hot soup and I hope that all who read it will enjoy it.

James Douglas Logan

J.D. Logan's official coat of arms

Foreword

This book represents the culmination of many years of research, debate and writing. A fascinating subject gave rise to an equally absorbing publication, which it is hoped will enlighten and give pleasure to countless readers. Part of its charm lies in the book's wealth of new material and its attention to biographical and other detail.

Logan's Way focuses primarily on J. D. Logan and Matjiesfontein, within the context of the host of interesting people, places and events of the age. Major John Buist has this to say about his legendary grandfather:

'My grandfather James Douglas Logan arrived in Cape Town with only a few shillings in his pocket. Due to hard work and determination he became one of the personalities of his time.'

Not only did Logan establish Matjesfontein and help to build the modern South Africa, but he made an even greater contribution to the nation and the world in setting a priceless example to others, in terms not only of what he achieved in life, but *how* he achieved what he did.

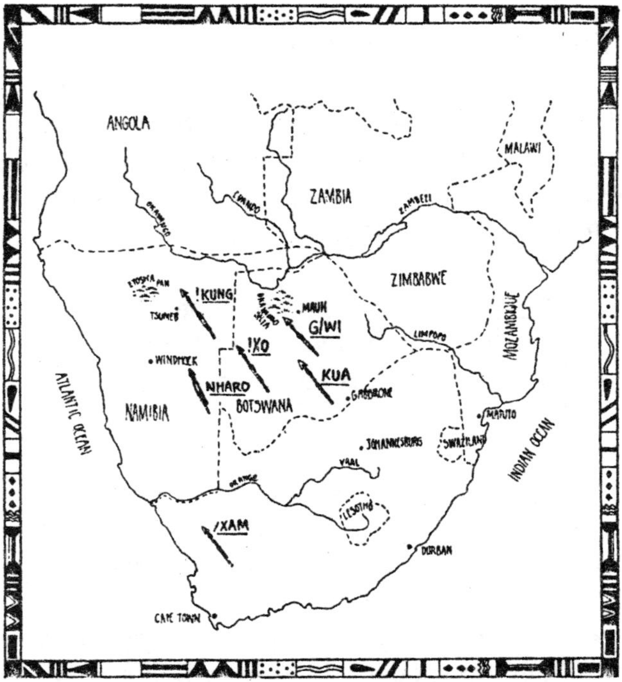

A map of southern Africa
indicating the principal Bushmen Tribes

The emptiness within is the great plain in our spirit where the aboriginal feeling of being known has been extinguished as we extinguished the Bushmen.

Laurens van der Post

THE KAROO

The name "Karoo" is derived from a Khoikhoi* word meaning "a dry place".

The Karoo is a vast semi-desert plain occupying some one-third of South Africa. It stretches from the top of the Hex River Pass to the Orange River and to the towns of Williston and Kroonstad. It forms the largest plateau of its kind outside Asia.

The rainfall being minimal, vegetation consists mainly of hardy, drought-resistant shrubs and succulents. Climatically, temperatures can vary in the extreme and are inclined to fluctuate, with very hot summers and bitterly cold winters (frosts in winter are commonplace, especially at night).

Even in summer, the fierce heat of day is succeeded by the cool of night. The land is criss-crossed by dry river courses, which can become raging torrents in a few hours and then, as swiftly, subside. The "flash flood" which struck the town of Laingsburg in 1981 claimed 103 lives and caused extensive damage.

Tragically, it just so happened that three rivers in the district, the Buffels, the Baviaans and the Wilge, all converged in flood at Laingsburg and there was simply too much water to be contained in the river beds.

It is believed that some 280 million years ago, the entire Karoo region formed part of a vast lake. It is famous for its fossils (perhaps being the cradle of

---

**The Khoikhoi are a nomadic Bushman tribe in Southern Africa who once roamed freely throughout the Karoo and other remote desert and semi-desert areas but are now much reduced in numbers and are confined mostly to certain parts of South Africa, Botswana and Namibia.*

Homo sapiens?) and is also renowned for its Bushman rock paintings.

This barren thirstland exercises an immense fascination for all who have experienced it; whether they have actually lived there, stayed awhile or merely passed through. From the clarity of the air, the stillness, to the wonderful shades of purple and blue that the hills take on in the early evenings, the night skies ablaze with stars, all of this leaves one with a sense of eternity.

CONTENTS

Prologue

It was a summer's night in October 1984, during celebrations held to mark the centenary of the small but historic village of Matjiesfontein nestling in the arid vastness of that strangely compelling part of South Africa, the Great Karoo. At this time South Africa was proving fashionable and was enjoying a revival of popular interest from overseas, especially in Britain, and Matjiesfontein (as it is now known) with its well-known turreted Victorian hotel, was crowded with visitors.

On this particular evening, Major John Buist, grandson and heir to that larger-than-life Scottish immigrant, James Douglas Logan, who had built the hotel in 1899, was entertaining friends to a birthday barbecue, better known in South Africa by the Afrikaans term, "braaivleis".

John Buist and his guests were gathered about the big, open fire which blazed cheerfully near a massive Australian bluegum tree, said to be the largest tree in the entire Karoo. The evening gave an impression of singular loveliness, as is so often the case in these parts of the world, cool and windless as it was at the end of a fiercely hot day.

The flickering coals, glowing with their promise of culinary delights to come, were enough to absorb much of the attention of the assembled guests. It was unlikely that any of these guests had ever given much thought to their link with Matjiesfontein's proud heritage. Yet evidence of the village's past glory, its closely-held secrets, lay all around. Nearby was the small cemetery which, down the years, had at once puzzled and intrigued travellers driving past on the long and tedious journey to and from Cape Town.

Some of the graves have indeed aroused particular interest among visitors to Matjiesfontein. One marks the last resting place of a distinguished British Anglo-Boer War hero, Major-General Andrew Wauchope, reputed to have been England's most wounded soldier. "The Gallant General", as history has remembered him, was the commander of the Highland Brigade in the Anglo-Boer War Battle at Magersfontein, near Kimberley. He fell, mortally wounded, in this battle.

The second much-visited memorial stone marks the grave of England and County cricketer, George Lohmann, who was invited by "The Laird", James Douglas Logan, a great lover of the game of cricket, to come to Matjesfontein, live in the village and play in The Laird's cricket team.

The third grave is that of The Laird himself founder of the village of Matjesfontein, farmer, politician, hotelier and so much else besides.

But now, at John Buist's birthday celebration, as the sun dipped below the distant horizon, guests were intrigued to see an unknown, kilted piper (by name Ian MacDonald!) march forward to stand before him. Buist acknowledged the salutation by himself coming to attention as the swelling sound of the pipes echoed far across the darkening Karoo. Then, clearly moved, he said quietly, 'The last time the pipes were heard here was at the burial of General Wauchope in 1899.' A somehow heroic moment had ended.

Another voice broke the silence. The softly spoken words came clearly through the Karoo night air. 'What about that other soldier? I wouldn't be surprised if he left his grave and walked tonight!' The remark brought a sudden lull and some of those present were seen to glance uneasily about them.

Tomb dedicated to General Andrew Wauchope

Reston Railway Station in Berwickshire Scotland around the time of J.D. Logan's birth - Logan senior was Station Master at Reston for some time

CHAPTER I

THE EARLY YEARS

The story of J.D. Logan and Matjesfontein (later to be re-named 'Matjiesfontein') can be said to have begun long ago and far away, in Scotland on a certain day in June 1871, when the headmaster of Reston House School, in the county of Berwickshire, north-east of the English border with Scotland, wrote a testimonial for his student, James Douglas Logan, junior. 'He is an excellent penman,' the headmaster writes, 'and a good arithmetician, besides being extremely smart and clever. I should rejoice to hear of him obtaining a good situation, and I have no doubt that he would discharge his duties to the satisfaction of his employers.'

Time was indeed to vindicate the confidence he had in his charge, on a scale undreamt of by the headmaster. He could hardly have imagined that James Logan was to become a man of wealth, power and distinction and that his destiny was to be played out in an Africa so distant from his beloved Scotland.

James Douglas Logan was born on the 26th of November 1859, in a modest house in Reston itself.

His youthful, formative years were steeped in a Scots 'no nonsense' family tradition handed down by his father, James Logan senior, who, like many of the simple menfolk at Reston, was employed by the North British Railway Company.

Otherwise, it was said of Logan senior that he was not beyond supplementing his meagre income with a little judicious poaching! There was no stigma attached to this; in fact, rather ironically, the reverse was the case in those days.

Predictably, young Jimmy and his friends soon became known as 'The Railway Children'. At the age of eleven young Jimmy ran away from home to join a sailing ship where he was employed as a cabin boy. It is said that on his first night at sea he was required to climb to the top of the mast! Jimmy spent three years at sea before returning to Reston, where he joined the Scottish Railways and became a clerk at the Rail Junction, a position once held by his father. In fact, the later family line which was to lead to Matjesfontein and the Karoo might well have been said at that early juncture, already to be apparent.

Logan's superiors at the North British Railway watched his progress in the company with some approval. He was marked for promotion.

But young Jimmy Logan's ambitions had by now far outgrown the confines of the River Tweed.

Within him he already cherished heady dreams of travelling to far places over the seas. Typically, he wasted no time in transforming his dreams into reality. He surprised everyone, including his employer and his parents, by resigning his post and then travelling to London with the intention of satisfying his need to see something of the wider world. The sceptics in his home town could hardly have been blamed for shaking their heads and remarking sagely that young Jimmy would soon be back, suitably chastened.

Mr. Arthur Shed, a local Reston man in his mid-nineties, wrote to the father of Mrs. Sheila Stoddart, a solicitor of Eyemouth, Berwickshire in 1971, upon her return from a visit to South Africa which included Matjesfontein. In this letter Mr. Shed records a somewhat different local legend concerning J.D. Logan's apparently hurried departure from Reston.

Mr. Shed writes:

'Mr. Logan's family in Reston were rabbit trappers and I remember that Mr. Logan apparently got into trouble with the police and was due to appear in court on charges of poaching. He disappeared before court proceedings and went to South Africa.'

A similarity between Logan's early life and that of Shakespeare?

The story may well be apocryphal, but what we do know is that "The Laird" was never deterred from returning regularly, over a period of years, to the vales of his youth.

Two countries which at the time were luring adventurous young men and women from their island birthplaces, were Australia and South Africa, and when on that cold February day in 1877, the vessel *Rockhampton* sailed from British shores carrying cargo and emigrants bound for Queensland Australia, young James Douglas Logan was one of those on board.

Whether or not it had originally been his intention to join his brother in Australia is not known, but when the *Rockhampton* was damaged in a storm in Simon's Bay off the Cape of Good Hope and had to put into harbour for repairs, James Logan took the opportunity to disembark from the vessel which he liked to refer to as "The Windjammer". Some sources have suggested that the ship was wrecked by a storm in the bay and that Logan was lucky to swim to shore in just the clothes he was wearing! Logan's discharge certificate, signed by the Master of the *Rockhampton,* is now in the possession of his grandson, Major John Buist of Matjiesfontein and Cape Town. While the manner of his arrival must remain a subject for conjecture, the records show that 19 year old James Douglas Logan first set foot on South African soil on the first of May 1877.

Subsequently, it was said that because he had only five pounds in his pocket at the time, Logan walked the more than thirty miles to Cape Town.

Though this story has never been confirmed, it stands to this day as yet another of the many legends which were to grow up around this extraordinary man throughout his entire life. His daughter Gertrude, latterly Mrs. Buist of Matjiesfontein and Cape Town, is adamant that he would have travelled by train to Cape Town from Wynberg, Wynberg at that time being the last station on the line. After all, Logan had been brought up with a railway background in that small town of Reston on the banks of the River Tweed, from whence he came. The likelihood is that James Logan would have been too practical to walk this distance when transport offered. Further, being a railwayman by family tradition, he would have wasted no time in establishing the possibilities of employment at Cape Town Station.

'That's for me!' he is said to have remarked to a friend when he first saw the already advanced stage of building construction at the new station. What his somewhat envious critics did not understand, was that Logan was a resolute young man who made his own decisions, and that these decisions were nearly always the right ones. This was to be the way of it all his life.

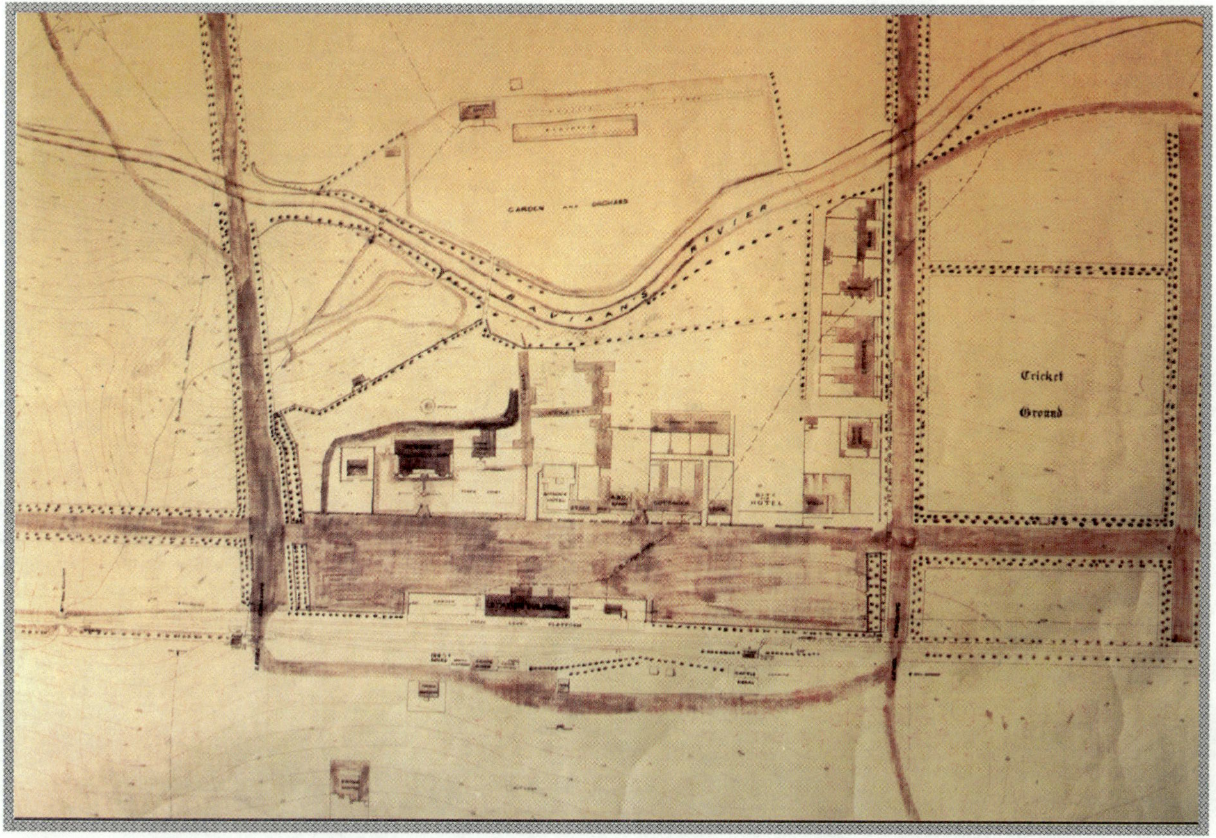

Map of the original Matjesfontein, as laid out by Logan

Matjesfontein Village in the early days

CHAPTER II

MARRIAGE AND A PLACE CALLED MATJESFONTEIN

Logan experienced no difficulty in obtaining employment at Cape Town station, by then nearing completion. Energy and a meticulous efficiency, combined with a certain flair for right action at the right moment, ensured that he rose swiftly, against keen opposition, to become Station Master.

He made such a success of this post that he was soon after appointed District Superintendent of the railway section between Hex River and Prince Albert in the Karoo. He was to be stationed at Montagu Road. With the arrival of the railways a small town began to grow up around the station and in 1883 the name was changed from Montagu Road to Touws River.

For Logan, however, the appointment carried with it an unexpected problem. The Karoo was isolated territory and the railway authorities, aware of this, decreed that the incumbent for the post must be married within three months of being appointed. This might well have dampened the enthusiasm of some applicants, but not that of Jimmy Logan.

Characteristically, he set about acquiring a wife. Jimmy made a proposal of marriage to a well-born young woman, Miss Emma Haylett, whom he had probably first met when she visited Cape Town from her home in the little farming town of Villiersdorp, some 70 miles from Cape Town. Thus Jimmy Logan became a member of the distinguished Haylett family, which originally hailed from Norfolk in England, but by then was well-established in Villiersdorp and Caledon.

Emma's father, Christopher Haylett, born in Norfolk, had married Catherina Maria Gertruida de Villiers of the farm Radyn at Villiersdorp. He was the proprietor of the very well-known White House Hotel in Strand Street, Cape Town, and it is more than likely that Jimmy Logan first met Emma whilst staying or dining at the White House. The hotel itself was famous for its curries! Many members of the Cape Legislative Assembly stayed there while attending meetings. A hitching-post used to stand on the pavement opposite what was then the hotel and what is now the Parkade.

When Logan was awarded the catering contract at Touws River, Emma must have seemed a very suitable wife with her hotel and catering experience! Logan also became very friendly with Emma's brother Pieter and with her father.

About this union a contemporary was to write:

'Mr. Logan was fortunate in drawing this prize in the matrimonial lottery. She was a true helpmate in the early days of hard work and worry, and she never failed to endear herself to those fortunate enough to be her friends.'

What were the thoughts of young Jimmy Logan from Reston and his even younger bride on that momentous day in 1879, as they travelled for the first time by train along the track that today still leads north-eastwards to the interior plateau of South Africa? The line even in those days threaded its way first through verdant valleys in which imposing farm homesteads nestled in lush farmlands on the lower slopes of the mountains. Sixty miles from Cape Town Jimmy Logan and his bride would have reached a small station called Hex River. From here the rail track became increasingly mountainous, twisting its way steeply upwards among craggy peaks, until suddenly the crags were behind them and they were moving through a strange semi-desert tableland covered with a variety of aloes and other succulents. A pitiless sun might well have shone on a landscape forged by time and fringed by distant, tinted mountains, mountains mutely proclaiming that they had stood thus for a million years. This was the Karoo.

What did Jimmy and Emma Logan make of this majestic, awe-inspiring sight as they stood there, hand-in-hand perhaps, on Touws River's Montagu Road Station – in the vastness of it, the strangeness?

The Karoo surrounded them, thousands of square miles stretching into the distance as far as the eye could see. It swept away in a great arc, reaching as far as Cradock in the Eastern Cape, Olive Schreiner's birthplace. She too, was destined to become a player in the Logan saga. Behind Jimmy and Emma as they stood there lay the ominously-named "Moordenaar's Karoo". They must have wondered – who *was* this murderer and whom did he murder? Or was it possible to believe that the Karoo itself might be the great destroyer? Mere fancy? The very nature of the Karoo lends itself to the fanciful, to ghosts of things past.

Meanwhile, Jimmy and Emma quickly adapted to the practical circumstances of living in Touws River. They found accommodation in the Frere Hotel, a simple Karoo hostelry, and Logan soon became refreshments caterer at Touws River Station.

Once settled in his new abode, Logan looked out over this wild and arid land, breathed in its clean, unsullied air, sweet indeed to one such as he, with a suspect chest, and decided he liked it. He was just twenty-one years old.

Logan now sought, and quickly found, his own wider personal horizon. Matjesfontein, a small station some 30 miles north of Touws River, immediately took his fancy. The environment appealed, the sense of eternal space.

He was quick to see the opportunities that would be presented by the ever-increasing upsurge of travellers through Matjesfontein by rail and dusty road, to the new-found diamond fields at Kimberley and the gold mines of the Rand. Always a quick decision-maker, Jimmy had soon negotiated the lease of the Frere Hotel, at that time the only hotel in Touws River. He followed this bold move by resigning from the railways.

The nearest railway halt north of Touws River was 'a place called Matjesfontein' as Logan later was to describe it. It consisted of little more than one solitary iron shed and a makeshift platform of loose Karoo stones.

Many of the locomotive drivers tended to increase speed to put the tiny stopping-place behind them as rapidly as possible. Nor did Logan give the station overmuch attention at first. He was content instead to survey the surrounding miles of Karoo landscape. Perhaps within him already were those first stirrings of the almost mystical compulsion that the Karoo was to cast upon him; or, was it simply as a contemporary, no admirer of his, was to remark sardonically at the time, that 'Logan was always to know a good thing when he saw it.'

And a good thing it proved to be. Land here sold at astonishingly low prices. Logan was able to purchase 3,500 morgen (about 7,700 acres) of land for four hundred pounds. This was the farm Visagie's Kraal. Henceforth, he would be able to take his horse rides across his own stretches of the Karoo. He would also bid farewell to an astonished community and residence at Touws River. The little town had served its purpose well. In a relatively short space of time, Logan had succeeded in making his mark. His name is reflected in Touws River today in Logan Street and the Loganda Hotel, which was in due course, to replace the old Frere Hotel.

Matjesfontein was from now on, to be the font from which he was to set out to make at once, a career and a fortune. In so doing, he was also to become an enduring legend. Jimmy Logan of Reston and Tweedside, had become the proud owner of 3,500 morgen in the Great Karoo, a property which included a zinc shed by way of a railway siding on the line from Cape Town to Johannesburg. This was 'a place called Matjesfontein' that few knew existed and still fewer ever visited.

Touws River had indeed been good to him. In addition to providing him with lucrative employment in the familiar world of railways, his catering enterprises at the Frere Hotel and the catering franchise at Montagu Road Station had opened up a whole new world of business activity for him. Against the prevailing background of a buoyant economy, he was well placed to take full advantage of the sharply increasing surge of railway activity as the iron road extended ever farther north-east towards Kimberley and Johannesburg.

His later experiences with the conventional railway catering franchise had revealed not only a considerable potential inherent in this sphere of operations, but had also provided him with a sound financial platform. A crucial element in his thinking now, must also have been his health. In the dry, hot spaces of the Karoo, the chest condition which had plagued him since childhood had all but disappeared and was not to trouble him again.

Above all, the Karoo had cast its magical spell over him as it had so many others. Jimmy Logan, looking about him at the dusty miles, had a very different perspective from that of a certain lady travelling across the Karoo, who is on record as having referred to the arid scrubland as 'this horrid place.'

The farm Visagie's Kraal which Logan purchased in 1885, lay about fifteen miles south of Matjesfontein. It was backed by a range of low mountains, the Witteberge, and was fronted by the highway from Cape Town to the north. At about the same time as acquiring Visagie's Kraal, Logan bought two adjoining farms: Besten Weg, which translates into "Best Way", and Pieter Meintjiesfontein.

It was on the latter property that, some years later, the famous memorial cemetery was to be established, a graveyard in which James and Emma Logan were themselves later to be interred.

The acquisition of three farms was seen by the local community and by Logan's friends in Cape Town, as a firm and final indication that he henceforth intended to make the Karoo his home territory. At the same time, the wandering Scot's affection for the traditional, the nostalgic, manifested itself once more – when Logan integrated the three farms into one, he chose to name the new property Tweedside, redolent of his beloved Scotland and the river of his childhood. Logan had by now successfully completed the merging of the three farms. Already the young man had earned a reputation for, as a local newspaper put it, making a success of every undertaking 'he turned his hand to'. Tweedside was to be no exception. Although he built a house on his farm he never did live in it permanently, preferring instead to entertain his guests there. His first love was Matjesfontein. His descendants live on Tweedside to this day.

What Logan wanted out of Tweedside was a paying farm, although there had never been any indication of underground water in any substantial quantity. Logan had however acquired some experience of Karoo soils and vegetation, which led him to believe that there was water underground, that the soil was suitable for crops and that it would sustain livestock. Local inhabitants were sceptical.

Logan's answer was to seek geological advice and on that advice, to sink a borehole on Tweedside and buy his own boring machine. Boring commenced in September 1886. Even the contractor was unconvinced that he would find any water and when the drill reached a substantial depth without success, the driller suggested that to continue boring would be a waste of money. This however, did not dovetail with Logan's philosophy of achievement. He ordered that boring be continued 'even if it took him through to Australia'. As usual, he was proved right! At six hundred feet, the drill struck a strong underground watercourse, water spurted out to a height of eighteen feet, and the situation was saved. This was the first artesian well in South Africa.

Two engineers from German South West Africa, now Namibia, were sent to Matjesfontein to investigate the drilling process. Two more boreholes were sunk and the future of Tweedside was assured. This successful outcome consolidated public opinion that Logan was a determined man who would succeed in whatever project he attempted. Copious water in the Karoo was news. The name of Logan was once more associated in the public mind with successful enterprise.

By the year 1893 there were more than five thousand sheep on Logan's farms, as well as cattle and other livestock. He succeeded in planting extensive orchards of many varieties of fruit trees, the most unlikely of these being cherries and pears. In addition, because the aesthetics of the Karoo had always been important to him, he planted ornamental trees to soften the harsh landscape. Australian gums were established to counter the prevailing winds which blew across the flat, rolling plains.

Logan's activities subsequent to his first visit to Matjesfontein clearly indicated that, after cautious beginnings, he had found the place in the Karoo that was to be his permanent home. Once having made this decision, he set about implementing his vision with a determined singleness of purpose.

The first step towards attaining his objective had undoubtedly been the earlier acquisition of the hotel and catering interests in Touws River. The securing of the railway catering contract at Montagu Road Station was, in the light of later developments, to prove of crucial significance.

However, an even more meaningful event had occurred on the 27th of May 1887, with the purchase of the freehold rights to the farm Bulhauer by Logan, for a consideration of only thirty-six pounds a year.

Not only did Bulhauer lie adjacent to Matjesfontein, but the farm also offered the additional advantage of three permanent springs, each yielding excellent water.

The reason why Logan bought this farm soon became apparent. The astute young man had been quick to realise that Bulhauer's close proximity to Matjesfontein, together with the abundant water supply on that farm, offered a fine opportunity for what might become a lucrative deal with the railway authorities at Matjesfontein.

Logan had observed that the water supply at this station was not only becoming increasingly depleted, such that it was unable to meet railway requirements, but that it was also of unsatisfactory quality.

This posed acute problems to government and local business interests, in operating a railway transport system already stretched to capacity and increasingly inadequate in serving transport requirements created by the burgeoning gold- and diamond mining industries of the Witwatersrand and Kimberley respectively. Again Logan moved with speed, precision and meticulous timing. He approached the railway administrators with the offer of a permanent water supply of high quality at Matjesfontein station.

This, Logan pointed out, would put an end to delays caused by locomotives shunting to other stations to obtain water, which was furthermore, very often of unsatisfactory quality. He offered not only to cede Bulhauer's water rights to the railways, but also undertook to organise the piping system which would lead water from Bulhauer to Matjesfontein.

Agreement was soon reached – effectively, the railway administration was to purchase the water rights on Bulhauer for two thousand pounds.

In a single transaction Logan had made profits far in excess of what he had paid for Bulhauer farm.

Indeed, this was by far the most profitable business venture he had embarked upon since his arrival in South Africa; it was to presage a number of other enterprises initiated by the canny Scot, each one pursued with relentless determination to a conclusion beneficial as much to himself as to others.

With hindsight, it was undoubtedly the Bulhauer transaction that marked Logan's crossing of a boundary, by which he signified his irrevocable commitment to the Karoo; indeed, it indicated that he was now ready to launch the beginnings of his great design.

The one exception to the pattern of successful enterprises, of which Bulhauer was the most recent, was to come later when Logan was awarded the famous, some would say notorious, but ever controversial, Cape Railways Catering Contract. But this debacle lay in the future.

'Matjesfontein' originally took its name from the reeds used locally to make mats. Around this rushy part of the Karoo a small settlement was to develop as far back as two hundred years before the advent of Logan.

By the time that J.D. Logan became interested in the place, a farm called 'Matjesfontein', owned by a former German soldier, had been long established.

The railway reached here in 1878, and on the first of February of that year the first "Iron Horse" came clanking and puffing into the makeshift new station. Then came J.D. Logan. He found water, planted trees among the stubby bush and transformed the station into an oasis. To quote an early visitor – 'Lo, the desert has blossomed into a smiling garden and the village is now a revelation to the stranger to whom before it was but a name associated with railway timetables, breakfast and dinner'.

The South African Railways – now known by the less romantic title of 'South African Transport Services' – have had a close and historic association with Matjesfontein Village ever since the then-new Matjesfontein Station was opened on the first of February 1878. Rail transport had been in the hands of a private company until the Cape Government took control in 1874 and began construction of a rail link to the north, to the "New Eldorado".

No other player in the South African story, romantic and exciting as it may be, can compare in terms of practical contribution, still less in terms of legend and romance, with the South African Railways and the role it played in the opening up of not only South Africa, but the entire African continent. It is a story that unfolds like a magic carpet of old across the tired, eternal hills of the South African landscape.

The first link in the chain of events that was to bind the railways indissolubly to Matjesfontein stands splendidly on display today in a place of honour on Cape Town Railway Station. This exhibit is the first steam locomotive brought to South Africa. It stands on extremely valuable mosaic tiles lifted from the concourse of the original Cape Town Station. The tiles are worked with the crest of the old Cape Government Railways. The engine was declared a national monument in 1936.

Popularly known as "William's Engine", this steam train was brought to Cape Town in 1859 and for many years thereafter was driven between Cape Town and Wellington by William Dabbs, who was brought from England specifically for that purpose. A photograph of him forms part of the display, and a splendid yeoman of England he looks too.

An interesting coincidence relating to Logan and the South African railway system, is the fact that the first sod of the railway line from Cape Town to Wellington via Stellenbosch was cut by Sir George Grey, the Governor of the Cape Colony in 1859 – the year of Logan's birth!

The Cape Town-Wellington line was started in 1859 under William George Brounger, later Chief Engineer for the Cape Government Railways. This was the first thrust to the North. The gauge was originally four foot eight and a half inches, as in England. However, it was later to be reduced for reasons of practicality, to the present three foot six inches.

Some say that this decision was made due to considerations of cost; others would contend that the wider gauge posed technical problems in traversing the formidable mountains.

The track reached Worcester in June 1876, only to confront the Hex River and the daunting Matroosberg mountain range. Yet the line was to forge ever-forward, snaking steadily up the Hex to Matroosberg Station at the top of the Hex River Pass and then on to Klein Straat, forty-two miles from Worcester.

From there the line wended its way across the wide Karoo, reaching Matjesfontein on the first of February 1878 and progressing beyond to Laingsburg in the same year.

From there the old Gibson and Red Star coaches set off on the five- or six-day run to Kimberley.

These brightly-painted coaches, drawn as they were by sturdy horses through Laingsburg's dusty main street and packed with eager fortune-seekers, gave that village something of the look of a Mid-West cowboy town. Later, as the line pushed northwards to De Aar (once called Broungerville) and beyond, the Iron Horse took over and stagecoach days became increasingly numbered.

At that time, when visiting Kimberley Logan would travel by train to the railhead at Fraserburg Road, then complete his journey by coach. At nightfall the coach would stop and the passengers would lodge overnight at nearby farms. Logan would relate the occasion when he, the farmer, the farmer's wife and the farmer's daughter all slept in the farmer's only bed, strictly in that order!

During the Anglo-Boer War the Iron Horse was to be used mainly for troop transport and for moving stores. The blockhouses, built by the British at key points to protect the northward track, still stand today as mute reminders of an historic service performed by those trains of earlier days.

The diamond discoveries were soon succeeded by an even more dramatic event. Indications of rich gold-bearing ore were uncovered on the Witwatersrand in the Transvaal and Johannesburg, almost overnight, was revealed as the centre of probably the richest goldfield yet discovered by man.

The rush was on!

The new goldfields presented an urgent need for a more comprehensive and efficient rail service to the interior. The Cape Government had responded swiftly to the new situation by buying out the privately-owned Railway Company and taking over the task of improving rail services. These improvements included the urgent construction of rail lines to the north, from the ports of Cape Town, Port Elizabeth and East London.

By 1884 these lines had converged on De Aar, many miles north-east of Cape Town. They reached Kimberley in 1885, which was coincidentally also Jimmy Logan's sixth year in South Africa. The "New Eldorado" beckoned, with young Jimmy Logan ideally positioned to carve his niche within it and by so doing, secure for himself a shining destiny.

All this was before the days of dining cars and Logan's next step was to obtain the concession for the railway refreshment rooms at Matjesfontein. He later opened Logan's Masonic Hotel and still later, the turreted Hotel Milner which was completed in 1899. Business boomed as more and more people were lured to the diamond fields by tales of fortunes made overnight; Logan was well on the way to fame and fortune. Meanwhile, by now Matjesfontein had become his favourite place and he and Emma soon went to live there.

A popular delicacy on the menu at the refreshment room at Matjesfontein was "Hot Logan Soup". A story current in Logan's time, perhaps apocryphal, told that Logan's soup was so hot that before passengers had had time to consume any of it, the guards were already blowing their whistles for them to resume their seats. We are left with the delightful picture of the train clanking out of the Matjesfontein station with wistful passengers peering out of the windows as they sadly inhale aromatic reminders of "Hot Logan Soup". Apocryphal or not, "Hot Logan Soup" still appears on the menu today of the present hotel at Matjiesfontein, now re-named the Lord Milner, but diners are given ample time to enjoy it!

It is a far cry from William Dabbs to the Blue Train, which today passes north and south several times weekly and stops at Matjesfontein three times a week in summer and twice weekly in winter. Passengers are indeed well catered for, but there are no stops for Logan's hot soup! Another speedy regular today is the Trans-Karoo Express and there are also many freight trains, mainly powered by electric units. The old steam engines of the past are no more than a memory, although occasionally the visitor does see a fine old restored "Iron Horse" in all its magnificence, ploughing smoke and whistle across the Karoo. Indeed, some visitors are even fortunate enough to experience the occasional ride in specially-arranged trains drawn by steam engines.

Today, as road transport has largely superseded freight trains, only about twenty trains pass through Matjesfontein every twenty-four hours, yet this is more than enough to keep alive the romance of the railway link with Matjesfontein that began in the nineteenth century. Logan steadily developed Matjesfontein until it achieved the elevated status of a much sought after, aesthetically charming village, health spa and holiday resort. Its fame spread and this tiny hamlet, set amid miles of stunted Karoo bush, became a favoured destination for famous people not only from South Africa, but the world at large.

At Matjesfontein Logan set about building an expansive house consisting of twenty-three rooms, including cellars, which he named "Tweedside Lodge", recalling his native Scotland. It was a fine example of colonial architecture and was further the first house in South Africa to benefit by electricity and other modern refinements. It was connected to Tweedside by what was at the time, the longest telephone line in the country. From here Logan was to create at once a business and farming empire, a career in politics, and his own unique niche in his adopted land.

In later life Jimmy Logan was to recall:

'Well, I began life at Reston Station, where after a few years I resolved on pushing my fortune in South Africa and accordingly set out for the Cape. I had few recommendations and less money and was just twenty years of age. I began at the Railway Station I well remember, as if yesterday. When I requested a situation, and received an answer that there were no vacancies at present, I went away hesitatingly and my procedure seemed to tickle the Inspector's curiosity. "What would you care to do?" he called after me. It was as if the opportunity had come. I said "Anything, provided it's not menial." A bit of waste was put into my hand and I began life cleaning buffers for thirty shillings a week. I was not long a porter; a station opened and the Inspector looked me up, "Could you manage a small station?" "Yes Sir, I can." "How do you know if you can?" "I know if other men can, I can." Bye-and-bye an Inspectorship offered itself ... and the promotion came my way ... but I cannot go on spinning my own yarn, as if no-one else had done the same and achieved bigger successes than I have. It was all done through hard work – work from early morn till late at night – a constitution that never tired, slept little; a disposition like Browning's hero "To never turn my back but march breast forward". That is all.'

Logan gradually acquired farms covering many thousands of hectares, but his favoured farm was always Tweedside. Today it stands on the National Road to Cape Town, about twenty kilometres from Matjesfontein. Down the years a multitude of motorists have seen the three imposing wrought-iron gates flanked by blue-and-white pillars, and many have wondered what romantic mysteries might lie behind the long lines of bluegums stretching from these gates to the distant hills. At Tweedside, Logan planted crops in profusion, including a wide variety of fruit trees. All this on land where few had presumed to plant before.

There is still today a nearby siding called Tweedside. In Jimmy Logan's day a special arrangement was made with railway authorities that would-be rail travellers to Cape Town from Tweedside would find a red lamp at the station. They would wave this as the train approached, thereby informing the driver of their presence, so that he would stop to take on passengers. Only the Union Express was exempt. However, in 1958 John Buist failed in his endeavour to stop the train by this means, perhaps like many before him!

Matjesfontein's heady days began in the 'nineties when the town became a fashionable spa and wealthy patrons from the capitals of Europe would visit, curious to see for themselves "The Village in the Desert".

Here Logan was king and here he held court. One of his more unlikely achievements was to bring London street lamps on ornate posts to the main street, which also served as the main artery to the exciting north. Those very lights still burn brightly under Karoo stars. Logan's visitors beheld them in amazement and then turned their curious eyes on Tweedside Lodge, home to the Logan and Buist families then and since. The visitor could also turn his gaze on the square building that stands in the grounds of the Lodge and read the unexpected words, "Karoo Steam and Wind Mill".

This building was used to grind corn and would further supply the village with electricity.

One of the first visitors to the village was Lord Randolph Churchill, whose son Winston was to achieve a fame even greater than his. The delightful picture emerges of the substantial figure of a somewhat conventionally-dressed English Lord plucking wild flowers in the wide Karoo in the spring of a bountiful flower year, wearing a spotless stiff white collar.

The partially-completed Logan's Milner Hotel, with its forecourt fountains sparkling in the Karoo sun, its famous turrets and ornate Victorian street lights, was to prove an irresistible attraction to tourists; meanwhile the ominous war clouds gathering at the turn of the century had the effect of turning the steady stream of great names into a veritable flood. Major John Buist, son of Logan's daughter Gertrude, recalls a hotel visitor's book – it has since sadly disappeared – that read 'like an international who's who.'

Why was so much of this, a microcosm perhaps, but undoubtedly a significant microcosm of a unique part of South African history in the making, destined to stem from a little-known Karoo village set in the marshes from which it takes its name?

Even the Matjesfontein mystique however, or the Matjesfontein experience as some have called it, does not explain why, at the turn of the century, so significant a stem of South African history had its origins here. What impelled the internationally famous Olive Schreiner to write much of her "Thoughts on South Africa" under a tree on a rocky hillside overlooking the tiny village? It was Olive Schreiner who later told Logan's daughter, Gertrude, 'I love Matjesfontein, it is my shrine.'

Matjesfontein, the tiny village which had for so long consisted of hardly more than a solitary zinc building in the Karoo, but which now boasted a fine new hotel, was destined almost overnight it seemed, to become famous not only in South Africa, but in the wider world, particularly in Britain. From here the high and mighty, including members of the British aristocracy, made the ocean voyages that were to bring a virtual flood of distinguished visitors to Cape Town. This in many cases was followed by the train journey over the Hex River Pass; a fashionable social "must". Matjesfontein increasingly became a familiar name in the salons of London and the stately homes of England. The great visitors book in Logan's Matjesfontein hotel was soon to be filled with the signatures of a number of distinguished men and women, as the cream of English society joined the throng determined to do the "in thing" by visiting that strange new hotel in the equally strange new village, in the place with the strange-sounding name. In smoking rooms of famous clubs throughout London, members would look up from their copy of the *Times* and remark to their fellow-members 'Matjesfontein? Damned outlandish name. In the *Karoo*, you say? Tell me, old chap, what the devil is the *Karoo*!'

Others among the distinguished foreign personages who visited Matjesfontein in that era were; the Duke of Hamilton, a young Sultan of Zanzibar, Admiral Rawson R.N., after whom the village of Rawsonville was later to be named, and that fine patron of cricket , Lord Hawke. South African visitors included; Lady Sprigg, wife of the then Prime Minister of the Cape, Cecil John Rhodes and Dr. Leander Starr Jameson, and of course, Olive Schreiner, whose indomitable eagle spirit was to be such an undefined but almost palpable presence down the years.

The politicians came largely because Logan himself was involved in politics to the extent that he was a Member of Parliament. A fellow-member and personal friend was Sir James Sivewright, Minister of Railways. Their association was to lead to the much-publicised Logan Catering Contract. But all of this lay in the future.

Matjesfontein village was unique when it was created more than one hundred years ago and the fame of this hamlet of authentic Victorian architecture had soon spread far beyond South Africa.

Many have sought to rationalise the Village's very special appeal. But perhaps the real secret of Matjesfontein's mystique lies in the apparent timelessness of the village and its surroundings, a sense of things past and above all, the brooding remoteness of the Karoo.

Photograph of Olive Schreiner aged 22 in Queenstown

CHAPTER III

OLIVE SCHREINER

The decade that saw the birth of Jimmy Logan at Reston in Scotland had also witnessed the birth four years earlier, of a small girl in faraway, emergent South Africa. This birth was at a place called Wittebergen, a mission station in the remote Karoo. Olive Schreiner was the ninth of twelve children of a German missionary. The destinies of Olive and Jimmy would soon come together and were to remain closely interlinked for much of their lives.

The catalyst for their friendship was the abiding love they both had for the great Karoo plains and for Matjesfontein in particular.

If Jimmy Logan can be said to have created Matjesfontein, it can equally be said that it was Olive Schreiner who was to bestow upon it its added lustre.

On the slopes of an uneven, rock-strewn kopje, that seemingly rises out of Matjesfontein itself, a lone tree attracts the eye; perhaps at first sight it would appear to be the only tree in a land of dusty plains rolling to distant horizons. Under the welcoming shade cast by its spreading branches, a metal plate affixed to the trunk tells the visitor,

'Under this tree Olive Schreiner wrote her book "Thoughts on South Africa".'

Olive Schreiner had by then already written the book which was to make her famous, "The Story of an African Farm", completed while she was still a young woman. Published in London by the house of Chapman and Hall, under the pen name "Ralph Iron", this book was to bring the young author enduring fame almost overnight. It also stands out as a catalyst, creating as it did a new dimension in South African literature.

Schreiner's life has been well chronicled from birth. She was born on the 24th of March 1855 on Wittebergen Mission Station in the Herschel district of the North Eastern Cape. Her father, Gottlob Schreiner, was a German missionary who had married an Englishwoman, Rebecca Lyndall. One of twelve children, six of whom died in early childhood, Olive was brought up in straitened circumstances. These circumstances caused her father to transgress one of the mission's cardinal rules – that no missionary should embark on any private trading. On his dismissal from the Church, causing his bankruptcy, the missionary's family broke up and Olive was placed with various families, living at first with her brothers and elder sister and helping with household chores. While staying with her brother Will at the diamond fields in Kimberley between 1872 and 1873, Olive had begun to write seriously. In 1874 she accepted the first of what were to become a number of positions, as governess to farmer's children in the Cradock and Aliwal North districts. She completed her first novel "Undine" in 1876, soon to be followed by her most famous work, "The Story of an African Farm".

Her great ambition had been to study and practice medicine, and with this in mind, she set sail for London in 1881 and upon arrival registered as a nurse probationer. Later she commenced training as a doctor but unfortunately her asthma was to prevent her from pursuing a medical career. Instead, when in 1883 at the age of twenty-eight, she had her novel "The Story of an African Farm" published, it brought her instant fame and an income which was to last Olive the rest of her life. London was a delight to her. She met and developed friendships with, many of the intellectual giants of her age, such as Eleanor Morse and Karl Pearson. She showed a particular interest in Havelock Ellis, with whom she developed a close friendship. Dr. Bryan Donkin made a proposal of marriage to her during this time, which she declined.

It was her unremitting enemy asthma, that was to drive her back to Africa and the Karoo. Olive had spent a total of eight years in England and Europe. In this time she had developed a strong social conscience and was later to become one of the first voices for feminism in South Africa.

Olive returned to Cape Town in 1889, staying briefly with her brother Will, but her health caused her to seek out a drier climate, and she decided to make Matjesfontein her home.

Here she was to lease a cottage, and in a letter to Havelock Ellis in March 1890 she was to write:

'I love the Karoo ... such a sense of wild exhilaration and freedom comes to me when I walk over the Karoo. This is a wide, long plain with one or two little kopjes in it. I am going to walk to one this morning. There are no farms or homesteads; the only place is this. It consists of the railway station, Logan's house, and a row of outbuildings or cottages of which mine will be one. There is not a tree or a bush in the mountain as far as the eye can see ... If only my asthma keeps away, this is the ideal place I have so been longing for.'

In a subsequent letter she reiterated this theme when she wrote to a friend, 'The Karoo is home to me.'

Olive Schreiner first lived in the hotel at Matjesfontein, but later moved to the small three roomed cottage known to this day as 'The Olive Schreiner Cottage'. The small village offered her what she most wanted; quiet, solitude and the Karoo. She writes, sitting in the shade of the solitary tree '... the air is dry and clear, so light that we draw a long breath to make sure we are breathing it aright. The stillness is so intense that you can hear the heaving of your own breast.'

It was at Matjesfontein that Olive Schreiner first struck up a friendship with Gertrude Logan, then only a young girl. Major John Buist has in his possession some of the letters she wrote his mother.

About this time, having been absent from Matjesfontein for some time, Olive writes in a letter to Gertrude:

'The train stopped at Matjesfontein for a while and I could see Tweedside and remembered the many happy times we have spent there but then I was suddenly sad, knowing that you were not there and that Tweedside stood empty.'

In another letter Olive Schreiner writes:

'I would be so glad if you could put a bath in my room and also, if you could do so without trouble, a desk with drawers like that old desk Jimmie lent me in my bedroom. It makes such a difference in writing if you have a large firm desk to write on.'

Portraits of the young Olive Schreiner show a woman of great beauty and vivacity. She was said to possess ‘lovely arms and shoulders’. Contemporaries described her as being more interesting than any of her creations, Lyndall, Rebecca, Bertie, Undine.

D.L. Hobman, in “Olive Schreiner: her friends and times”, writes:

‘She never invented any character so dramatic and fiery, so perverse and inconsistent as her own. She was everything that was contradictory; a self-centred altruist, an individualistic socialist, an aggressive pacifist; she abhorred war yet most vehemently supported the Boers against her own countrymen; she denied God while all her life her soul was penetrated with awareness and love of the Divine.’

It was “The Story of an African Farm” that proclaimed her importance as a new writer, and a great many public figures including Cecil Rhodes proclaimed her talent. On her return to the Cape, Olive had been ‘more solitary than you can conceive’ she wrote in a letter to Havelock Ellis in 1890. And a little later, ‘I think if I lived fifty years in Africa I should never make one friend.’ Then ‘... there is one man ... Cecil Rhodes, the head of the Chartered Company (The British South Africa Company) whom I think I could like if I should meet him; he’s very fond of “The Story of an African Farm.” ’

Olive probably first met Rhodes in June 1890, after he had become Prime Minister of the Cape Colony. She was invited to travel to Bloemfontein in his party in December 1890, for the opening of the new railway line and thereafter was to dine at Groote Schuur often. Rhodes reciprocated by visiting her at Matjesfontein on several occasions.

She writes of him, 'He is even higher and nobler than I had expected but our friends are so different we could never become close friends.'

In a letter to W.T. Stead written when Rhodes was visiting Mashonaland Olive says, 'Any accident to him (Rhodes) would I believe mean the putting back of our South African development for fifty years...'

Olive's subsequent disillusionment with Rhodes possibly began in 1891 when Rhodes voted in the Cape Parliament for the "Strop" Bill, authorising the corporal punishment of black servants.

In her turbulent life Olive Schreiner was to know many intense joys and sorrows. At the age of 38 she married Samuel Cronwright, a farmer from Cradock. As a result of her strong feminist convictions they exchanged names, becoming respectively Olive and 'Cron' Cronwright Schreiner.

The death of her baby after just twenty-four hours of life was an unforgettable grief. A macabre story current at Matjesfontein is that Olive Schreiner had the bodies of both her baby and her dog placed in small coffins which remained with her in her room.

A close but tempestuous friendship was to develop between Olive and Cecil John Rhodes (it is said he once left the train at Matjesfontein for no reason other than on a sudden impulse to converse with her).

However, the Cronwright Schreiners were both ardent supporters of the Boers in their struggle for independence, causing them to become critical of the Charter Company and its activities in "Charterland" and of Cecil John Rhodes himself.

Olive is on record as saying in an interview:

'Nothing is more difficult than to arrive at the truth of things in Rhodesia. There are people enough who have communicated with me and all these people are afraid of Rhodes and Company.'

She continued that her informants on this subject had stipulated that they must not be named:

'All these people are mortally afraid of Rhodes, even for their lives.'

She added:

'Rhodes has the millions and if he ever succeeded in laying his hands on Johannesburg then a reign of terror would soon prevail as in Kimberley and Rhodesia.'

At Matjesfontein an historic confrontation between Olive and Rhodes was to take place.

Cronwright Schreiner writes of the incident:

'The end of personal intercourse came when Olive refused on the Matjesfontein Station to shake hands with him and Sivewright because of a transaction between them concerning the price of Government ground – at Matjesfontein, I think – a "deal" which she had held to have been flagrantly and shamelessly dishonourable!'

The Jameson Raid brought Olive's antagonism towards Rhodes' policies to a head, and resulted in her writing "Trooper Peter Halket of Mashonaland", a violent indictment of the British South Africa Company's activities in Rhodesia. In a letter, Olive wrote that this book had cost her more than anything else she had ever written.

There was great tension aboard the *Dunvegan Castle* in 1897 when Cecil Rhodes and Olive and Cron were fellow-voyagers to England: Olive and Cron with the manuscript of "Trooper Peter Halket" and Rhodes en route to give evidence to the Commission of Enquiry into the Jameson Raid.

Olive Schreiner's "An English South African View" was written in May 1899, a few months before the outbreak of the South African War. It was a vain appeal to the Imperial Government to hold back from war. Her pro-Boer sympathies were well known – she attended a meeting of ten thousand people at Worcester in 1900 in protest against the war and during the war years between 1899 and 1902 she was at times confined at Hanover under martial law.

But it was the asthma which had bedevilled Olive for so many years which was to precipitate the breakdown of her marriage to Cron. Desperate to alleviate her condition, Cron sold his farm and changed his profession. He and Olive moved from one place to another over the years; from Kimberley to De Aar and then on to Johannesburg and Hanover in search of a suitable climate.

In 1906 she wrote to her 'Dearest Gertie', Gertrude Logan about a planned visit to Matjesfontein as follows:

'My heart has been troubling me and I think the rest and quiet of dear old Matjesfontein will do me good.'

Olive spent the years from 1913 to 1920 in England and Europe. She was effectively trapped in England during the war years, necessitating a lengthy separation from her husband Cron. Olive was devastated by the 1914 war and became so depressed that her projected great novel "From Man to Man", on which she had worked for some forty years, would not be completed.

Two years after the Great War the Cronwright Schreiners were reunited in London. Cron hardly recognised her when she opened the door, so weak and ravaged by illness had Olive become. She left for South Africa, alone, in 1920. In her last letter to Cron Olive wrote:

'One day I will go up to Matjesfontein just for one day, if I can find anyone to take me.'

Three months later Olive Schreiner died alone in a boarding house in Wynberg. She was interred in 1921 in a tomb constructed of ironstone boulders on the mountaintop called Buffelskop, near Cradock, about 650 metres higher than the surrounding plain. Her baby and her dog Nita were buried with her in separate coffins. It has been said she chose her own burial place when she stood on the mountaintop with her husband Cronwright Schreiner some twenty-five years earlier. The site overlooks the farm where she wrote "The Story of an African Farm".

Olive herself had undoubtedly decided that Buffelskop's bleak majesty, so in keeping with her own "brooding and eagle spirit", was an eminently suitable last resting place.

Olive Schreiner was indeed a woman of many parts, writer, feminist, and staunch protagonist of women's enfranchisement. She was also an avowed and determined pacifist – criticising Gandhi for acting as a stretcher-bearer for the English against the Boers, saying that a true pacifist will never take part in war at all. She was a complete liberal, fiercely in favour of racial freedom for all. Her concern for the African formed part of her concern for humanity. She felt an urgent need for the total reconstruction of South African life.

As far back as 1912 she predicted that if Africans were denied the fullest opportunities to make a valid contribution to the country as a whole and were compelled to work in limited areas, it would be South Africa's ultimate undoing. If most of the country's inhabitants had no stake in land or share in government, she reasoned 'Can we ever know peace?'

Olive herself said 'It never pays the individual who speaks the truth, but it pays humanity that the truth should be spoken.'

It is astonishing that there seems to be no memorial in South Africa to honour one of her greatest daughters.

From her own letters we know also that there was a part of her that was forever Matjesfontein.

Olive Schreiner (centre) pictured with her parents at left and younger brother William Philip Schreiner

Emma and James Logan of Matjesfontein

CHAPTER IV

LOGAN THE MAN - THE 'LAIRD OF MATJESFONTEIN'

At Matjesfontein a growing local populace had already conferred on J.D. Logan the unofficial title, 'Laird of Matjesfontein'. In part this was undoubtedly a tribute to his Scottish heritage, although the more disgruntled of his acquaintance would suggest that the accolade had originated from Logan himself. Whatever its source, there is no doubt that the title pleased him mightily; and it was as 'The Laird' he was to be popularly known for his lifetime even though, on the 18th of June 1897, he was offered a much higher sounding award: a 'baronetcy'. The occasion was one of those local Matjesfontein concerts which had already become famed far beyond the borders of the Karoo. A local theatrical celebrity, by name H.A. Campbell, who had taken the chair at the concert, remarked that he had only accepted the chair 'because it affords me the opportunity of calling on Mr. Logan, the wizard of Matjesfontein'. 'Truly,' Campbell continued, 'it takes no one less than a wizard to turn the barren Karoo into a veritable garden. In fact, Mr. Logan might be honoured with the title, 'Baron Karoo'. The report continues that, after laughter and applause, J.D. Logan 'appeared on the stage and his performance of numerous sleight of hand tricks was clever to say the least of it. Mr Logan was encored to the echo. Mr. Logan, in response, proceeded to produce two-shilling pieces and half crowns from the whiskers of gentlemen in the audience, and from the hair styles of the ladies'. This encouraged the chairman to remark, 'Why be poor when money can be had so easily?' This was in the *Worcester Advertiser* of June the 6th, 1897.

However, Logan was content to rise no higher up the 'honours' tree than 'simply a Laird'.

Of the private man himself we know rather less. We do know that he was dynamic, precise, energetic and ambitious. There are the portraits; moustachioed, high-collared, impeccably and conservatively dressed. We also see that he was a family man, devoted to Emma and to his children James and Gertrude. Although he lived until 1920, he was essentially a Victorian, and there is no reason to assume that he was immune to the peccadilloes of the Victorian male. He also had an eye for the ladies. However, all we do know about him on this subject has been written by others. The Laird does not speak for himself. This adds a touch of mystery to the legend. John X. Merriman, at a farmers' meeting, said that he wished that there were ten thousand Logans in South Africa. And Cecil Rhodes is on record as saying he had only met two creators in South Africa, one being himself and the other J.D. Logan.

As to the reason why Logan had sought out Matjesfontein, the answer was essentially the climate. Logan, who like Rhodes suffered from a weak chest, benefited so much from the exhilarating a dry climate that he was completely cured. He was also quick to perceive that overseas doctors were recommending Beaufort West as a health resort at a time when, in Europe, many families had kin suffering from tuberculosis, or consumption as it was called then. The victims continually languished and often died of consumption, in fiction and in fact.

It was Logan who succeeded in establishing Matjesfontein as the prominent health and holiday resort that it became.

Matjesfontein was J.D. Logan's pride. He ensured that the buildings were in immaculate condition, the streets in front of the houses as clean as a ship's deck. A Mrs. Maritz who lived at Matjesfontein for many years and who knew Logan well relates that the streets were swept regularly. She says that should any inhabitant leave rubbish, paper or weeds in front of his or her dwelling, Logan would knock on the offender's door to demand that the alien items be removed, and would usually deliver a short lecture as well. This meticulous neatness was surely inherited from his Scottish family background.

In spite of his strictness Logan was well-liked. He did not distinguish between rich and poor; and colour made no difference to his treatment of people.

He was also known for the immaculate neatness of his personal appearance. Every morning while at Matjesfontein he would walk by the houses of his village beautifully dressed and wearing a dress shirt and a flower in his buttonhole. He would then go to the station to wait for the passenger train, greeting people with a graceful wave of his walking stick.

He used to converse with the passengers, and treated the engine driver and stoker to cups of coffee while they waited for the travellers to finish breakfast.

Logan served two breakfasts, one at three shillings and sixpence where travellers went for quieter, more high-toned society, and a half-crown breakfast for other customers.

An example of his forward thinking was a plan he had to establish a school of railway cooking at Matjesfontein.

Another successful enterprise was the Matjesfontein mineral water factory. Here he made soda water, lemonade and ginger ale for thirsty travellers.

Two days in the year were of special significance at Matjesfontein; both November the 26th, Logan's birthday, and New Years Day were celebrated lavishly.

The entire community was en fête and liberally treated at long tables which were sumptuously laden and sheltered under railway tarpaulins.

Young and old, rich and poor, gathered together and Mrs. Logan would make sure no-one was overlooked.

After the repast all present were obliged to take part in the races; winners and losers alike received prizes from Mrs. Logan herself at the end of the day and the Laird would watch each presentation with great pleasure.

Though he demanded their best of them, Logan delighted in doing what he could to make his employees happy.

Logan had an undoubted talent for friendship. At one birthday celebration William Souter, M.A., wrote a delightful tribute to his great friend, Jimmy Logan.

This went in part:

'Here's to ye Laird'

'Here's to ye, Laird! Rax owre your han'
To get the grup ye unnerstan'-
Guid guide ye an' a' your concerns!
May ye be spared to see your bairns
Grow up weel fav'red, healthy pair,
Free frae the pangs o' pain and care,
Twa saplin's strong' the Scottish pine
That grace your Native Land an' mine.
Here's to ye, Laird! Let's hear you views
On rinderpested stirks an' coos,
On duties, taxes, wages, rent,
And on the present Government
Sae may your joys last thro' your life,
An chief o' a' – your kindly wife.'

Key to Scottish dialect:

"rax" – reach
"Guid" – God
"bairns" – children
"weel fav'red" – well favoured
"frae" – from
"twa" – two
"stirks" – bullocks
"coos" – cows
"sae" – so

Meanwhile Logan's children were growing up, a part of this exciting world. (Jimmy junior was born in 1880, and his sister Gertrude in 1882.)

J.D. Logan was a loving husband and father. Letters to Emma, when he was overseas without her, evince great affection for "My own darling wife" and "My darling Tibbie". Logan enquires fondly about her well-being and that of the children – how he longs to be back with them at Matjesfontein!

Gertrude and Jimmy, in common with many country children of that era, were initially educated by governesses. Gertrude was then sent to Rustenburg School for girls in Cape Town and must have been one of the earliest pupils at the school which had opened its doors to pupils in 1894.

Young Jimmy was later enrolled at Blair Lodge School in Scotland.

At 6.00 a.m. on Friday morning the 26th of September 1895, J. D. Logan wrote from the Waterloo Hotel in Edinburgh:

> '...while I sit writing Jimmie is lying in bed next to the table fast asleep. (Yesterday about 3 o'clock)...(we) spent an hour or two with Mr. Gray. He talks very highly of Jimmie and gives him a splendid character and says that throughout he has been a very good boy and never has any illness. The school commences on Tuesday and I will take him there myself and see that he is all right. As soon as the places are open we are going out shopping as there are a lot of things that the wee chap requires. I only wish I could get someone else to do it as I hate shopping.
>
> I remain, my dearest Tibbie,
> Your ever loving
> Dadda
> XXXXXX'

The names Jimmy Logan gave to his favourite farm and to his residence, Tweedside and Tweedside Lodge, give some indication of his great love for the land of his birth. And not only the land but the people of that land had a very special place in his heart. Most of his employees were at one time connected with the Scottish Railways. Moreover, his private secretary, S.M. Wright, his accountant, W.J. Mason and another staff member, a Mr. Kitchen, all hailed from Aberdeen. Eye Bank Cottage at Matjesfontein served as their office.

Mrs. Mason, who was living at Touws River in 1952, thought very highly of her late husband's former chief and spoke of the good treatment they had received from the 'proud old Scot'.

One young Scottish engineer, James Stoddart, from Berwick-upon-Tweed, came to South Africa in April 1893 on board the *Dunottar Castle;* almost immediately on arrival in Cape Town, he made his way to the Royal Hotel to keep an appointment with J.D. Logan, to whom he had a letter of introduction. J.D. Logan gave him a hearty welcome. Stoddart relates:

'As we were talking, a gentleman passed down the street and Mr. Logan stopped him and spoke to him. He was Low, Superintendent of the Cape Railways. After that Mr. Logan and I went straight down to the Superintendent's offices and they at once engaged me to go to Bloemfontein to the railway shops there. There was no particular room for any more men but Mr. Logan is very powerful, and has a great deal of influence out here. I went round to Mr. Logan's hotel and got a letter of introduction to the manager at

Bloemfontein and a free railway pass for myself and luggage. I leave Cape Town on Wednesday night in the same train as Mr. Logan who is going to Matjesfontein. A gentleman in the 1st class in the *Dunottar Castle* on hearing I proposed going to Mashonaland offered me a good amount for a report of the various prospects of electrical engineering there ... I have to see him in Johannesburg in three or four weeks from now ... I of course, am very thankful to Mr. Logan for his very kind efforts, and told him so, but I propose to take the best chance offered irrespective of by whom it is offered.'

In the letters James Stoddart wrote to his parents in 1893, he referred many times to Mr. Logan who had taken him under his wing. Sadly, this promising young Scottish engineer was to die some eighteen months later, possibly of a fever, far from home.

The first electricity-generating windmill built in South Africa, seen at front of Logan's house (Photograph by courtesy of James Walton)

J. D. Logan's headstone

George Alfred Lohmann

George Lohmann - rest in peace

CHAPTER V

J. D. LOGAN AND CRICKET IN SOUTH AFRICA

The game of cricket was first played in the villages of Surrey in verdant Southern England about the beginning of the year 1598. The players in these early games of the noble sport were encouraged, some say inspired, by the interest in the game shown by Henry VIII and Edward VI. From here the game spread to other English villages where it was played by princes and publicans alike. Later Frederick, Prince of Wales, became attracted to the game.

J. D. Logan's deep affection for cricket undoubtedly helped to popularise the game in South Africa. It was he who brought the game to Matjesfontein. More than an enthusiast, Logan seems himself to have been a fair performer on the cricket field.

A succession of distinguished cricketers were enticed to these southern climes by Logan's almost fanatical devotion to the game. Lord Hawke's team came to South Africa as a result and George Alfred Lohmann, England fast bowler, was brought here at the personal invitation of J. D. Logan himself.

Probably the first official game of cricket to be played at Matjesfontein commenced one fine morning in November 1889 as part of celebrations to commemorate the opening of the Matjesfontein Water Works.

The match was played on hard Karoo soil, with

bluegum trees throwing shadows over the unforgiving pitch, surrounded as it was by ubiquitous Karoo bush against the backdrop of the purple Witteberge.

Logan had invited a large number of guests including many dignitaries, among others Lady Sprigg, wife of the Prime Minister, Colonel Schermbrucker, M.L.A., and other leading politicians, who arrived by train in the morning. As well as cricket, Logan had arranged rifle shooting, pigeon shooting, billiards and tennis to entertain his guests.

Shortly before lunch Lady Sprigg performed the opening ceremony by turning the wheel and lo! a fountain sprang into the air. The Worcester band played for the assembled guests and, according to a newspaper report 'The luncheon provided in a decorated railway shed would have done credit to a first-rate London hotel.'

Logan became a generous supporter of local cricket. He arranged the two visits by Lord Hawke's teams to South Africa, in 1894 and 1896, and of course they played at Matjesfontein! Some interesting team portraits of those matches still hang on the walls of the Laird's Arms at Matjesfontein. He also arranged and financed some of the first South African cricket tours to England. The first tour that Logan took to England, in 1901, was referred to in the press as, variously, Logan's cricket team, the South African team, and "the Colonials".

George Alfred Lohmann was said by many to be the greatest cricketer of his generation. Most of Lohmann's spare time after leaving his school, the Louvain School in Wandsworth was devoted to playing cricket. At the age of eighteen he was invited, and accepted, an offer to play professionally for Surrey, which was a great honour.

George Lohmann was described by a contemporary critic as 'a first class bowler, splendid field and a dangerous bat' and from 1884 to 1892 there was hardly an English cricketing victory in which Lohmann was not involved. It was a severe shock to the cricketing world when at the age of twenty-eight, Lohmann was found to be suffering from tuberculosis. He was ordered abroad in search of a cure, and arrived at Cape Town at the end of 1892.

From January to May 1893 Lohmann stayed with Logan. His health restored, he returned to England, but ill health again sent him Karoo-wards in the hope of making a full recovery.

Lohmann was quoted in the Cape Argus of the13th of September 1893 in an interview in Cape Town as saying:

'Mr. Logan and I are going off tonight to Matjesfontein were I shall stay long enough to get acclimatized, afterwards proceeding to Kimberley and Johannesburg. My headquarters will be on the Karoo, the air of which is the best I have ever breathed!'

Mr. Lohmann continued:

'Mr. Logan's kindness has contributed in a great measure to my health being as near restoration as it is at present. He has a most genial heart and is one of the best sportsman - in the proper sense of the word - in the world.'

In reply to a question Lohmann went on 'my chief delight was being in the cricket field and in 1884 I was asked to play for Surrey ... During the three consecutive seasons 1888, 1889, 1890 in first class matches I obtained more than two hundred wickets each season ...

His health began to show visible signs of improvement almost immediately in the crisp pure Karoo air and he had apparently fully recovered when he returned to England in 1894. He played again for Surrey in 1895 and 1896 and also took part in the Gentlemen versus Players matches.

A report at the time said 'No-one played cricket more strenuously or threw himself more completely, heart and soul, into the game - Lohmann allowed himself no respite.' After experiencing differences with the Surrey Club and suffering another flare-up of tuberculosis, Lohmann decided to return to South Africa.

While in Johannesburg, he was employed by the Water Works Company. Lohmann was coach at the Wanderers Cricket Club and also played there as an amateur. He only remained there for one season as his health began to trouble him once more.

Jimmy Logan, a true patron of the game of cricket if ever there was one, on hearing of Lohmann's breakdown, offered him a home at Matjesfontein and with it the post of assistant manager of the South African team. He would also assist in arranging for visiting British teams to play at Matjesfontein. Lohmann gladly accepted.

Although once more the clean Karoo air effected a temporary improvement in Lohmann's health and served to prolong his life, he found it impossible to spare himself where cricket was concerned, and sadly in 1901 Lohmann died a bachelor in Matjesfontein aged only thirty- six, to be mourned by the entire cricketing world.

His impressive tomb, surmounted by an engraving in stone of a cricket bat and a cricket ball symbolically breaking the stumps, is at once a moving tribute to a great cricketer and a monument to the game of cricket in the unlikely environs of the Karoo.

The inscription on the tomb reads:

'This memorial is erected
by the Surrey County Cricket Club
and friends in South Africa
in memory of one of the greatest all-round cricketers
the world has ever seen,
a bowler of infinite variety
a splendid field and a resolute batsman,
he did splendid service for Surrey from 1884 to 1896
as well as for the players and for England.
His whole heart was in cricket
and he played the game from start to finish'

Upon his arrival in England on the fourth of August 1894, Logan was interviewed on the subject of the First South African Cricket Team then in England.

Logan, one of the original guarantors of the tour, had withdrawn from the guarantee list of the team, and when asked about his feelings on the matter said:

'I found myself dealing with people with whom formerly I had had no negotiations on the subject of the guarantee and with the fact that the team would visit England under quite different Management to that which I had been led to anticipate. When I, the original guarantor promised my five hundred pounds it was on the distinct undertaking made of course with Mr.

Cadwallador that the very best team ... should visit England ... I had in fact two reasons for my action in withdrawing from the list. I contend that had it not been for Mr. Cadwallador as Secretary of the South African Cricket Association, there would have been no visit of a team to England at all, and further I found myself on the end without any voice in the question of management ... Hendricks ought to have been included in the team; he was their finest bowler, but they would not have him because he was a coloured man. Yet I observe that since they began their tour of England they have played against colour, and therefore I ask myself why they could not have played with colour? ... and whether a man is white, black or yellow makes no difference to me nor does his particular trade or profession. What I want to see is the crack player and the crack sportsman.'

On being asked if he were a near neighbour of Olive Schreiner at Matjesfontein he replied 'Yes, I am. Three weeks ago last Sunday she was staying with her husband at my sanatorium. I believe she is engaged in a new work, needing much more thought and labour than her later brochure.'

To a question regarding Karoo life and its health-giving qualities, Jimmy Logan replied:

'Well, I should prefer not to say too much on that point, as you know I am an interested party owning as I do the Matjesfontein Sanatorium, the only one in the Karoo. No, I should prefer not to say anything as it might look as if I were puffing my own wares.'

In March 1896 at Matjesfontein, Lord Hawke's team played against a Colonial team brought together by Logan from all over the Colony. The *Cape Argus* reported that the lavish hospitality which was shown towards the guests was doubtless destructive of any very brilliant cricket! The *Cape Argus* continued its description in this vein:

'... Mr. Logan himself was the life and soul of his team and kept them at it with utmost perseverance. When the game was over dinner was served in sumptuous style and the evening passed merrily amid the popping of champagne corks, the warbling of songsters and the speeches of friends.'

The *Cape Argus* went on to quote Lord Hawke on the cricketing issues of the day.

'Lord Hawke touched on the question of professionalism ... and on the position of Dr. (W.G.) Grace. With regard to the latter he said that in whatever way he might be looked upon in any part of Her Majesty's dominions, at home they looked upon him as far above anybody else, the greatest cricketer that the world had ever seen and whose like they would never see again ... In this country, he concluded; they had done their best to uphold cricket in the way of amateurism, but he hoped that when a team was sent to England it would be representative of South African cricket and there would be no humbug about it. The Laird got to his feet and poured out his soul on the thorny question of professionalism. He maintained that as soon as a gentleman went and received money for his services he was a professional ... If a man was a cricketer he could still be a gentleman and a professional and he had the greater respect for the man who went honestly forward and received the money at the front door, than for the man who received it at the back door.'

Several songs were sung and the evening passed in the most festive manner. It was not by arrangement that the up train was two hours late, but it was admittedly a fortunate circumstance, and no-one growled at the Cape Government Railways.

Third English Team in South Africa 1895 - 96 Back row (l. - r.) E.J. Tyler; Sir T.C. O'Brien; A.M. Miller; T. Hayward; G.A. Lohmann. Second row (l. - r.) C.B. Fry; Hon. J.D. Logan; Lord Hawke; C.W. Wright; C. Heseltine; A.J.L. Hill. Front row (l. - r.) S.M.J. Woods; H.R. Bromley - Davenport; H. Butt.

J.D. Logan pictured with some of the industrialists and railwaymen of his day, marking the occasion of Mark Twain's visit to South Africa

CHAPTER VI

THE RAILWAYS CATERING CONTRACT CONTROVERSY

Perhaps the cornerstone of Jimmy Logan's fortune was laid on the first of October 1882 when, aged twenty-three, he opened his first catering operation at Touws River. In 1877 there were only two railway refreshment places, one at Klapmuts and one at Wellington, which the Railway Administration hired out at one pound a month.

From that time onwards the railways expanded rapidly until five years later there were 102 stations and 962 miles of track; there were also 19 catering places at intervals along the line. A Mr. Louw had obtained the contract to sell refreshments on Matjesfontein Station. He probably had little more than a coffee stall, as in fact Matjesfontein Station itself was in 1884 hardly more than a zinc shed.

On March the first 1884 the contract was taken away from Louw and a new contract was drawn up with J. D. Logan. Logan erected a new refreshment room at his own cost and paid an annual rental of seventy five pounds to the railway administration until the end of April 1885.

From May the first 1885, a significant date in the Cape Railway Administration, all passenger trains included a kitchen to provide food for passengers. The kitchens at that time could not completely replace the refreshment rooms, but they provided strong competition. As a result the railway administration reduced the rentals for various catering places, Touws River's rental falling from one hundred and fifty pounds to seventy-five pounds and Matjesfontein's from seventy-five pounds to thirty-seven pounds.

The De Aar catering enterprise was reduced from one hundred and fifty pounds to one hundred pounds. De Aar was obviously a busier and more lucrative proposition.

By 1887, 123 stations had been opened, of which 23 offered refreshments. Logan was now caterer at Touws River, De Aar and Kimberley Stations. In January 1893, over a distance of 3353 track miles including 175 railway stations, there were 45 catering places or coffee stalls, of which 10 were managed by Logan.

It seems clear that Logan's aim was to eventually control all Cape Railway catering stations.

A contract for each catering enterprise was drawn up between the General Manager of the Cape Railways and the tenant concerned, after tenders had been asked for in the public press, to be submitted in writing by a specified date, with the final choice to be made by the General Manager. The tenant undertook that the building would be used solely for catering purposes, which would be carried on satisfactorily. Contracts were usually granted on a five-year basis. The larger catering establishments usually offered strong drink and it was the responsibility of each tenant involved to take out the necessary license according to the relevant Act, The Liquor Act No.28 of 1883. Each tenant was also responsible for furnishing and equipping the rooms, such furniture and equipment remaining the property of the tenant.

The tariff had to be approved by the General Manager of the Railways. This tariff ensured certain protection against exploitation of passengers and was in line with general prices elsewhere. When passenger trains arrived at catering places at meal times the timetable usually allowed for a 45-minute stopover. In such cases the tenant was obliged to serve both hot and cold meals. Tenants of the larger refreshment rooms were allowed to open an hour before the passenger train's arrival and to close one hour after its departure.

There was a stipulated amount of money for which two people had to stand surety should the tenant fail to pay his rent.

Until 1893 J. D. Logan had followed the proper procedure in tendering for his contracts. All contracts until 1886 were limited to periods of five years. From 1886 onwards, Logan was given the option of renewing his contract for a further five years if he so wished.

Ohlssons Cape Breweries benefited a great deal from these licensed catering places and in many cases the directors stood surety for the contracted rentals. All but one of Logan's contracts were guaranteed by Ohlssons directors.

In 1890 the Railways determined to erect new buildings at Matjesfontein, which J. D. Logan would have to use for his railway catering business. On this account a new contract had to be drawn up and Logan, whose contract was about to expire in any case, hastened to conclude the new contract. This was formally signed on the 17th of May 1890 by Logan and the General Manager, C.B. Elliott, with the option of renewal for a further five years.

Logan seemed to be less interested in the smaller coffee stall enterprises, but took out licenses at Bloemfontein, De Aar, Kimberley, Kroonstad, Matjesfontein, Naauwpoort, Orange River, Touws River, Fourteen Streams, Vryburg and Worcester, all of which stops supplied alcoholic beverages.

The Railway Administration issued Logan with free tickets on the trains, and from 1890 his manager S.M. Wright was included in the concession. This enabled Logan to visit his catering places with ease and to make sure his employees were carrying out their duties to his satisfaction.

The Cape Government had been responsible for the construction of the railway line up to the Vaal River at Viljoensdrif and thus had control over the Free State line till 1897. For this reason Logan was able to contract for businesses in the Free State as well. Logan built the refreshment room at Kroonstad for a sum of five hundred pounds, finishing it on the 18th of February 1892. He thereafter managed it at a rental of eighty-four pounds a year.

The extent of his catering contracts (he ultimately controlled more refreshment rooms than any other tenant) and his travelling concessions caused Logan to become well known in business circles and to wield a great deal of influence with regard to railway timetables, which he would presumably have arranged to suit his catering enterprises.

The railways formed a substantial source of revenue for the Government of the Cape Colony, this revenue consisting of freight rates and passenger fares, rentals from catering rooms, import duties and customs tariffs. However, the competition from the newly-formed Transvaal and Natal catering franchises was severe. The incomplete Delagoa Bay and Natal railway systems were progressing fast and although the Cape Railways presently had a monopoly of freight and passenger traffic to and from the goldfields, this could not last. Cape Railways needed to provide a better service to ensure travellers would prefer them to any other railway network. Further, this could have an influence on whether overseas travellers would end their voyage at Cape Town or Durban.

It was the task of Sir James Sivewright, Minister of Railways, to implement improvements. He imported new railway coaches and improved the heating facilities on trains. The catering services were not deemed satisfactory and investigations were set in motion to rectify the situation. One school of thought held that all catering should be put under the direct control of the railways, which should create a catering sub-department and appoint its own managers, to run these enterprises and share in the profits. The General Manager of the Cape Railways, Mr. C. B. Elliott, was in favour of this solution.

However, Sir James Sivewright considered that it would be unwise to burden the railway administration with any more responsibility in this regard. He was strongly of the opinion that the best alternative would be to employ one single tenant as manager of all railway catering. This tenant would have to be a person of extreme capability and he must surely have had J.D. Logan in mind. Sivewright said later to the Select Committee 'I quite shared the opinion that if we put all refreshment rooms under one management, then Logan was the best man'. His feeling was that Logan's rooms, though leaving room for improvement, were far better than any of the others.

C.B. Elliott also considered Logan to be the best manager and when Logan went overseas early in 1892, Elliott suggested Logan should investigate catering enterprises overseas with regard to possible adoption of their methods by Cape Railways. Elliott's idea was that Logan should be the General Manager of a catering sub-department of the railways.

To give the monopoly to another manager would have caused great difficulties with regard to Logan's many options and tenancies.

On September the 13th 1892, Logan met Elliott and Sivewright in Cape Town and proposed that all the catering places on the Cape Railways should fall to him and he was asked to put his proposals in writing. In his letter, referring to his overseas tour, Logan explained that he felt that it was absolutely essential for all the catering services on the railways to fall under the control of one management. Among other things, he wrote that matters were at present satisfactory neither to travellers nor himself and that reorganisation was very necessary. Should his application be successful, he suggested all tenants should receive twelve months notice of cancellation of their contracts, unless the terms of the contracts precluded this.

Logan would pay an additional two hundred and fifty pounds over and above the specified rentals for the first five years, once the catering places were put in his name; five hundred pounds per annum for the next five years, and one thousand pounds per annum thereafter for the following five years if he wished to renew his contract again.

Sivewright then wrote to Elliot 'I am quite prepared to authorise the railway refreshment rooms arrangement as sketched out today in the interview between Logan, you and myself and you can intimate this to him. But the details cannot be settled offhand, and in view of all the papers being at any time called for in Parliament, I wish to have the whole business in writing.'

This contract, which awarded to Logan complete control over all the railway catering places, fulfilled the adage "easy come, easy go". The contract, according to procedures laid down, should have been put out to tender; although Logan was the obvious choice, the flouting of established legal codes was to have a disastrous effect on the Government of the Cape Colony. The local press soon became involved in the controversy and once more demonstrated its power and influence. An abbreviated report of this contract appeared the day after its signing, in the *Cape Times*. As the news slowly filtered through, tremendous consternation and dissatisfaction ensued, especially among the existing railway tenants, particularly as the newspaper report omitted to mention the twelve-month notice clause or that tenants would probably be permitted to manage the rooms they presently held. Logan said he felt so strongly in favour of having one general manager in charge of all the railway catering services, that should the railway administration appoint someone they considered more suitable, he would be prepared to give up his tenancies.

The contract Logan obtained gave him sole catering rights to existing establishments as well as any other places which might be established with the extension of the Cape Railways. No extra rental was mentioned in the contract for any such expansion of his catering facilities. The options he was granted gave him control for almost twenty years (otherwise the contract followed the usual guidelines). This gave him great influence over any elected government in that period and there being no effective competition, could well lead to his dictating the methods and standards of catering.

C.B. Elliott as General Manager and J.D. Logan signed the contract, and the three managers of Ohlssons Cape Breweries each signed surety for two-thousand-five-hundred pounds.

Logan now controlled 36 catering establishments, large and small, in the Cape Colony and the Orange Free State. The total rentals excluding the extra amounts agreed to in the new contract came to three-thousand-six-hundred-and-sixteen pounds.

The existing tenants were notified of the new contract after the 19th of October 1892 and were informed as to when their tenancies would expire.

Dismay and dissatisfaction were rife among tenants, and rumours spread rapidly. John X. Merriman, on hearing of the contract in this manner, brought it to the notice of Attorney-General J. Rose-Innes. As neither minister had any official notification they dismissed the matter as mere speculation.

On November the 4th the Logan contract was sent to the Secretary for Finance to ascertain the correct amount payable in terms of stamp duty and the revenue stamps which had to be affixed thereon. This seemingly trivial detail might well be described as the catalyst which set in motion the chain of events that was to reverberate through the political life of the Cape Colony and further afield.

The stamp duty amounted to two hundred pounds and two shillings and had to be affixed to the contract within twenty-one days. But this was already overdue, resulting in a fine of four hundred pounds and four shillings. The Secretary for Finance suggested the date of the contract be amended, but the Attorney-General said the date could not be altered and that the whole contract must be redrawn first and thereupon stamped within twenty-one days.

During the parliamentary recess, which commenced on the 29th of August, Sir James Sivewright and Prime Minister Cecil Rhodes visited Kimberley, Johannesburg and Pretoria, and on October the 5th they both journeyed to England. P. H. Faure (Secretary for Native Affairs) and J. W. Sauer (Colonial Secretary) were meanwhile respectively visiting their constituents on the Border and the Eastern Province.

John X. Merriman and J. Rose-Innes were as a consequence the only Cabinet Ministers remaining in Cape Town. No cabinet meetings could be held during September and October, so only a few Ministers were aware of the contract which Sivewright had awarded to Logan. But on November the 4th 1892 the *Beaufort West Courier* carried this item:

'It is reported that the "cute master of Matjesfontein" has obtained a monopoly of all the refreshment rooms on the railways from Matjesfontein to Johannesburg. The chief cause for doubt is that we have seen no notice calling for tenders, and we do not like to think our present Government capable of perpetrating a job like this, leading as it would doubtless do, to the injury and discomfort of the travelling public. People complain that Logan – fine fellow as he is – is too much to the fore in these matters, and if this wild rumour should prove true, there will indeed be murmurings loud and deep throughout the land.'

Rose-Innes sent a copy of the report to the Assistant General Manager of Cape Railways, A.W. Howell, who had furnished Logan with his list of catering establishments, to find out if the report were true. Howell reported the account to be correct. He offered to show the Attorney-General the contract and sent him all the correspondence appertaining to the Logan Contract, being unable, himself to explain why tenders had not been asked for, and why Sivewright had acted without prior consultation with his colleagues.

Rose-Innes then sent a telegram to Sauer, before discussing the whole matter with Merriman. He also wrote a letter to Rhodes in which he expressed his strong feelings against the way in which the contract had been awarded without it going through the offices of the Attorney-General, as was normal procedure, adding that the contract itself had been very badly constructed. He asked Rhodes to let Sivewright know that he expected him to furnish a complete explanation of the manner in which the deal had been concluded.

The whole matter was given great prominence in the newspapers. In a letter to the *Cape Times* on November the 8th 1892, one correspondent suggested, 'If tenders had been asked for a much higher tender could in no way have been unlikely and the railway income could have been so much greater.'

The *Midland News* of the 11th of November illustrated the plight of present lessees, who would be made redundant by the provisions of the new contract:

'... it is whispered that the lessees of both Cookhouse and Cradock – not to mention the smaller fry along the Midland Line – have received notice to quit, and this is taken as a positive sign that the octopus grasp of the Laird is to be still further extended. It is rather rough on the lessee of the Cradock Refreshment Room, after struggling away for years in a shanty that would be a disgrace to a Russian railway line, he should be hustled out just when the department have woke up to the necessity for a new building. But then, we suppose, poor Liddell has no friend at headquarters to square matters for him.' No official statement had yet been made.

Sauer and Faure returned to Cape Town immediately on receipt of Rose-Innes' telegram. As deputy leader in Rhodes' absence, Sauer cabled Rhodes on behalf of his colleagues in the cabinet to demand the immediate cancellation of the Logan Contract.

Rhodes and Sivewright replied immediately by cable, to the effect that Sauer and his colleagues had full authority to act as they saw fit, but that the issue had been thoroughly investigated by the departmental heads.

Sauer, Merriman and Rose-Innes remained adamant in their belief that the contract was not in the public interest and they therefore replied by cable:

'Cabinet thinks contract must be cancelled. Ask

Sivewright wire Logan that effect. Reply.'

On receipt of this cable Rhodes gave instructions for the contract to be withdrawn.

J. H. Hofmeyr, Member for Stellenbosch, and D. Graaff had by now approached Rose-Innes to send an official cable to Sivewright. The Attorney-General cabled the following message:

'Hofmeyr, Graaff say Logan contract causes grave dissatisfaction. Weakens ministry. Place friends false position. Show Rhodes.'

(Blue Book A3 1893 L. Contract.)

Sivewright omitted to show Rhodes this cable, so Rhodes was only informed of Hofmeyr and Graaff's feelings when he returned to South Africa.

Immediately on receipt of Rhodes' cable, Sauer contacted Elliott and asked him to proceed with the cancellation. Elliott sent a short note to Logan informing him that the contract, which had granted him the monopoly of railway catering places, was being withdrawn.

No reasons were given in the note but Elliott subsequently despatched a cable intimating to Logan that he would discuss the matter next day at Matjesfontein. However, Logan did not receive the telegram in time to be able to meet Elliott.

Elliott then sent Logan a further message suggesting that he and Logan should discuss the matter with Sauer in Cape Town.

Sauer and his colleagues were well aware that the cancellation of the contract could cause severe repercussions. Elliott reported to Sauer that he had heard that Logan intended bringing a claim for damages of fifty thousand pounds against the

Government for the withdrawal of the contract.

Sauer, Merriman and Rose-Innes were of the strong opinion that whatever the cost the contract should be withdrawn, as the effects of retaining the contract would do far more damage.

On the 29th of November 1892 Logan lodged demand for fifty thousand pounds against Commission of Crown Lands and Public Works breach of contract, or that the contract should reinstated. The Government was given until the 5th of December 1892 to answer the claimant.

The Railways appointed the firm of Reid and Nephews to defend the case. Had the Government offered to pay Logan compensation at the outset it is possible the whole matter would have been settled amicably and not gone to trial. Logan's lawyers were Van Zyl and Buissine. They instructed Advocates P. Schreiner and M. W. Searle to act on his behalf. Reid and Nephews instructed Advocates S. Giddy and W.S. Webber to act on behalf of the Railways. The case was scheduled to be heard on May the 31st 1893.

Sivewright returned to South Africa on the *Dunottar Castle* on April the 25th 1893, still of the opinion that the contract was in the general interest. He advised the government's legal representatives, the day before the case began:

'... I am very anxious to enter the witness box and finish all the information in my power relating to it'.

Yet this would have been impossible, as Sivewright was himself a member of the government against whom Logan was bringing his case.

The preparatory examination was concluded on the 13th of March 1893. The case for the claimant was opened by Advocate S. Solomon Q.C., who gave a synopsis of the claim and the basis on which the amount of the claim was assessed; this being the annual profit of more or less seven thousand pounds which Logan assessed the contract should have been worth to him.

In conclusion Logan would have asked fifty thousand pounds for the contract should he have wished to sell.

Advocate Solomon said that it was obvious damages must be paid and the point of issue was the amount.

The Attorney-General was also of the opinion that damages should be paid, however, he considered two thousand pounds to two thousand six hundred pounds to be a fair compensation in view of the fact that the revenue from the catering places was not constant and that some places had even, historically, showed a loss.

Chief Justice de Villiers in his summing up, taking everything into consideration, such as that catering places even showing a loss must be kept open in terms of the contract, agreed that Logan was entitled to damages which should not be set too high. He said Logan was still a young man and could tender again for the catering places he had lost through cancellation of the contract.

The verdict of the court was that five thousand pounds should be adequate compensation and that the defendant should bear the costs of the case.

Young James Stoddart coincidentally was on the *Dunottar Castle* on that same voyage that brought Sir James Sivewright back to Cape Town. In a letter to his parents dated the 25th of April 1893 he wrote:

'Mr. Logan is very busy about his court case just now and had very few minutes to spare today but I will have a long talk to him on the train going up'. (to Bloemfontein)

On the 29th of April James wrote from Bloemfontein:

'I travelled on the same train as Mr. Logan to Matjesfontein which we reached at eight 0' clock in the morning and had breakfast in the refreshment room. Mr. Logan took me round to his house which is close to the station, and gave me a letter to the District Superintendent here who is a personal friend of his. The house Mr. Logan built here is a very pretty one and has all the latest appliances such as electric light, telephone, etc. In fact Matjesfontein is the prettiest station on the whole line and only consists of the station, Mr. Logan's house and flour mill and some other small cottages. Mr. Logan is a large man out here and has a great deal of influence.

He is coming to Scotland on the boat leaving May 31st, and you will see him. The great case in which he is suing the Government comes off in two weeks and he expects to win it. I have heard several outsiders talking about it in the hotel we stayed at in Cape Town, and the general opinion is that the Government will get a showing up. I dare say you will hear before this letter reaches you how it has gone as they will probably cable the news to London.'

Then in a letter home written on Sunday June the 4th, James Stoddart remarked:

'I see Mr. Logan has won his case and has received five thousand pounds and costs. He has not been up this way yet as far as I am aware.'

Thus for Logan the matter had come to a more or less satisfactory conclusion; he had five thousand pounds in his pocket and could still tender for any catering place that became available, whilst retaining all those refreshment places which were already contracted to him.

Gertrude Logan in her younger days

Karoo House

CHAPTER VII

DOWNFALL OF GOVERNMENT

Yet for Rhodes, the outcome was fraught with peril. He had succeeded Sir John Sprigg as Prime Minister of the Cape Colony and formed a government on the 17th of July 1890. His cabinet consisted of a coalition of highly talented men.

However, their ideological differences made for a very fragile situation. Sir James Sivewright and P. H. Faure were members of the Afrikaner Bond, and Rhodes was in agreement with them with regard to their agricultural policies. However, John X. Merriman, Sauer and Rose-Innes disagreed with the Bond, particularly regarding its Native Policy.

When at the beginning of Rhodes' period of governance J. Laing brought a motion 'That in the interests of the Country it is impolitic and undesirable that the official representative of the British South African Company should be the Prime Minister of the Colony' (Hansard 1890), the Bond members gave Rhodes their full support, support which was to continue until the Jameson Raid of 1895. The Bond in 1891 requested a change in the Parliamentary Franchise, which was the precursor to the Franchise and Ballot Act of' 1892, tripling property qualifications for the vote from twenty-five pounds to seventy-five pounds. This would have the effect of disenfranchising many Africans. Merriman, Sauer and Rose-Innes, who all championed the cause of the non-European franchise, opposed the bill. Sir James

Sivewright and John X. Merriman were frequently at odds with each other, this being yet another case in point. Merriman's resentment of Sivewright sprang in part from the role Sivewright would invariably play as right-hand man to Rhodes, acting in close communication with him in attempting to implement Rhodes' great schemes.

Sivewright also loyally supported the Bond in most instances, particularly in relation to Native land rights, whereas Rose-Innes openly declared himself to be in favour of individual land ownership.

The Logan contract, coming at the critical moment in local politics that it did, was enough to act as catalyst, tearing apart the delicate fabric of the coalition government.

The cancellation of this contract however, did not satisfy the three anti-bond members, Merriman, Sauer and Rose-Innes. In February 1893 in a letter to his mother Merriman wrote 'The Logan business of course renders it quite impossible for me to sit in the same Cabinet with a man (Sivewright) who could do such a thing as well as others which have come to my notice. As soon as Rhodes returns, an explanation must take place which will probably end in my resignation.'

Rhodes returned from overseas on the 8th of April 1893. On his return the triumvirate of Merriman, Sauer and Rose-Innes made it clear to him that they could not sit in the same Cabinet as Sivewright.

This put Rhodes in a great dilemma. His overseas visit was concerned with negotiations to purchase Delagoa Bay from the Portuguese to prevent the South African Republic under President Paul Kruger from having access to a mutual port. Sivewright had helped enormously with these negotiations. Rhodes needed the backing of a strong cabinet in this proposed purchase. Merriman, Sauer and Rose-Innes were a very able trio and Rhodes was loath to lose them. However James Sivewright was invaluable to him, closely involved as he was with all Rhodes' plans and having the Afrikaner Bond on his side.

The Prime Minister did all he could to reconcile Sivewright, Merriman, Sauer and Rose-Innes, travelling himself between Sivewright's home and meeting the others. He was convinced a compromise could be reached. However as days passed and the impasse remained, Merriman advised Rhodes to let the Governor hear of the cabinet crisis and ask him to return from Kimberley where he was on a visit. Rhodes then told Merriman that he (Rhodes) would tender his resignation to the Governor, Sir Henry Loch, and would recommend that Sir John Sprigg be asked to form a Government.

On his return Sir Henry asked Rhodes to approach Merriman, Sauer and Rose-Innes once more to change their minds. However they proved adamant and Rhodes went to tender his resignation. 'Onze Jan' Hofmeyr had advised Rhodes to resign and then himself form a new cabinet and Rhodes followed this advice.

Rhodes had invited J. T. Molteno to Groote Schuur to discuss the crisis with him. Molteno expressed his own view very strongly by saying that if Rhodes were going to get rid of Merriman, Sauer and Rose-Innes, whom he considered wholly in the right, for Sivewright, then he (Molteno) would support the three Ministers. And this was the end of Molteno's loyalty to

Rhodes. He never again set foot in Groote Schuur.

Rhodes' new Cabinet was thereby deprived of four very capable men. The new Cabinet Ministers were Sir John Sprigg, J. Laing and William Philip Schreiner (Olive Schreiner's brother).

However, Merriman, Sauer, Rose-Innes and Sivewright were still members of the Legislative Assembly. Rhodes would be obliged to explain his actions in constituting a new Cabinet in Parliament. Inevitably, in so doing he would have to make public all the details relating to the Logan contract and the ensuing crisis in the Cabinet.

The Logan Contract debate began in Parliament on the 19th of June 1893, and on the very next day Sir James Sivewright introduced a motion 'that all the papers and correspondence connected with the Logan Contract respecting railway refreshment rooms of date 14th September 1892, be laid on the table of the house'.

This motion met with approval from those members who were ignorant of all the facts of the case; each member was to be provided with printed copies of all the correspondence.

Hofmeyr proposed that the whole matter be referred to a select committee, which would discuss inter alia the future policy of Government towards public catering services.

After much heated discussion as to who should serve on this select committee of five members, the House eventually agreed that the members should be nominated by the Speaker. The select committee so nominated consisted of J.H. Hofmeyr (Stellenbosch), P.J. du Toit (Richmond), L.A. Vincent (George), T.E.

Fuller (Cape Town) and J.M. Orpen (Wodehouse).

Sivewright's amended motion eventually read:

'Ordered; - That the papers and correspondence connected with the Logan Contract, respecting Railway Refreshment Rooms which have been laid on the table of the House, be referred to a select committee, consisting of five members, to be nominated by Mr. Speaker, for enquiry and report on the questions involved, and more especially as to the most desirable system to be adopted in future in dealing with the catering for refreshments on Government Railways, the Committee to have power to take evidence and call for further papers.'

Most of the Press reports of the time were largely in favour of the formation of the Committee.

For elucidation of what the words 'questions involved' meant, the Committee consulted the Speaker. According to the Speaker who, on the 12th of July 1893 read the details to the House, it was laid down 'that the Committee could firstly, only consider and decide upon the wisdom or advisability of executing the contract in question; and secondly, on the effect or consequence of such a contract. But no enquiry could be entertained in regard to the personal integrity, honour or character of any individual Member of the House. Such could only be considered on specific charges or articles referred to a Committee specially chosen to consider the same, the duties of which would be of a judicial nature, and no such function is assigned to this Committee'.

The Select Committee was thus very limited in its investigations, and there was no possibility of determining any question of malpractice. The Select

Committee conducted interviews with, in particular; Sivewright himself; Member of the Legislative Assembly for Griqualand and ex-Minister of Railways, C.B. Elliott the General Manager of the Railways, Howard and Difford, his joint Assistant General Managers, as well as H. Attridge, whose mother was the tenant of the Cape Town refreshment place, J.D. Logan and many others, to ascertain their opinions on the cancelled contract and the catering service in general.

On August 14th, the report of the Select Committee was made available to the Lower House. The report set out in detail the whole history of the Logan Contract and concluded that the best way to conduct the catering situation was indeed to place it under the management of one person. However, it disapproved of the manner in which the Logan Contract had been undertaken and also objected to the longevity of the contract, which made no allowance for changes in circumstances and tariffs. It also noted that the contract was deficient in that there was no mention of extra rentals for possible new refreshment rooms.

The Committee recommended that the Cape Railways should divide its catering services into three departments, namely, the Eastern Cape, Western Cape and Cape Midlands. As the tenancies expired the General Manager should call for tenders for each section for a period of not more than ten years. The Committee also recommended that any existing lessee should be able to tender for any of the franchises in the various departments as they became available, possibly with Logan in mind.

The conclusion the Committee reached was that

the Contract was not in the public interest and that they supported the views of Merriman, Sauer and Rose-Innes in this respect.

An article in *The Kimberley Independent* dated June the 3rd, 1893 reported:

'The Logan case, which everyone declared was coming in like a lion, has gone out like a lamb. The case was to be a Cause Célébre. Everyone was agog to see what would come of it. All kinds of political secrets were to be revealed. Sir James Sivewright it was said was to be put in the box and invited to swear to all manner of facts or negations of fact. Well what has happened?

Mr. Logan has come into court claiming fifty thousand pounds damages. The Court has admitted his right to claim damages ... but has fixed the amount awarded at one-tenth of the amount claimed ...'

In many press reports and letters to newspapers at the time there emerged a strong feeling that the contract had been in the public interest and was fairly drawn up and that Merriman, Sauer and Rose-Innes had seized on it as a way of embarrassing Sivewright at the expense of the hapless taxpayer.

Although in some press reports it was recommended that the three be reinstated into the Cabinet after their unfair treatment, the complications of such reinstatement would have caused even more trouble and the matter was left to rest.

Parliament then debated the five thousand pounds awarded by the Court to Logan. After a great deal of discussion the House voted in favour. The Attorney-General informed the House that including costs the amount payable to him would be six-thousand-and-fifty-six pounds and this was approved.

The discussion of the report took place on September the 7th and the House unanimously agreed to Hofmeyr's motion that the report should be adopted so that Government could consider the whole matter.

Logan and Sivewright, whose actions had caused these great political upheavals, emerged with their reputations intact. In fact, in Logan's case all the considerable publicity that the case had engendered, only served to make him better known.

On October the 19th the *Argus* reported 'The Logan contract we maintain was not the real cause of the dissolution; it was only the match employed to ignite the fuel which lay heaped up in large quantities.'

Sivewright and Merriman were never the best of friends; both had aspired to obtain the post of Agent General in London, which remained a bone of contention between them.

Rhodes had not only lost some credibility, but had also, in more practical terms, lost part of his political support base; the case had resulted in the resignation of four influential, capable and valuable supporters in Sivewright, Merriman, Sauer and Rose-Innes.

His break with Molteno also caused him considerable loss. In the crisis that confronted Rhodes on his return to Cape Town, he contemplated relinquishing his leadership of the Colony and even went so far as to suggest to Lord Chief Justice de Villiers on the 28th of April 1893, that de Villiers should form a cabinet in which he (Rhodes) would be prepared to serve. However, while de Villiers was preparing the list of Ministers to form his Cabinet, Rhodes met with Sprigg, who promised Rhodes his full support in a second Rhodes ministry. It was only through the newspaper that de Villiers learnt that Rhodes was busy preparing to serve again as Prime Minister. Not surprisingly, this caused Rhodes to lose yet another good friend and adviser. The ramifications were vast. Had Rhodes been able to continue to command the respect and loyalty of the all the wise and capable men he once had, perhaps the Jameson Raid might never have taken place - perhaps, perhaps?

This refreshment contract which caused such consternation and so many upheavals was brought to finality in November 1895 when the Government awarded Logan the contract for the Western system as far as Vryburg and the contract from De Aar to the Vaal River via Naauwpoort. It covered about 1700 miles of track and Logan was to pay four thousand two hundred and fifty pounds per annum for it. The main refreshment outlets were Cape Town, Matjesfontein, Beaufort, Victoria West, De Aar, Kimberley, Vryburg, Naauwpoort, Springfontein, Bloemfontein and Kroonstad. A certain Mr. Charles Green obtained the Midland contract and Mr. W. H. Courtnay the Eastern Line.

(Railway note: - November 1895 - A traveller on the train from Cape Town to Johannesburg wrote 'We observed an incident which proves our Post Office Department is quite "up to date". On a small siding a lad held out a post bag and although the train was going at considerable speed, the Post Office clerk in the van caught it!')

Emma Logan in full regalia

CHAPTER VIII

WIDER HORIZONS – POLITICAL LIFE

By 1892 Logan had become an important figure in the Cape Colony and it was not surprising that public life should have beckoned him. He became a Justice of the Peace for the Achter Hex River area in that year. Admission to Parliament soon thereafter was a natural progression. In 1894, after the upheavals of the Logan Contract had subsided somewhat, and backed by his friend and Afrikaner Bond member Sir James Sivewright, Logan once more made himself available as a candidate for Worcester in the General Election of 1894.

The sitting Member was J.M.P. de Villiers, the M.P. for Worcester for the past fifteen years, who had beaten Logan soundly in the previous General Election.

The Worcester Chronicle reported on nomination day the 26th of January 1894:

'Mr. Logan's appearance on the platform was greeted with vociferous cheering. Among other things he paid moving tribute to the late Mr. de Vos, one of the two previous members, whom he had ever regarded as an upright gentleman and a worthy representative of the' Electoral Division of Worcester. He told the voters that though he was no pure Afrikaner, he was a corn farmer and a sheep farmer. His interests were therefore identical with those of the electorate. He said the Worcester railway station was a standing disgrace and should he be elected he would do all in his power improve the situation and see that Worcester got its fair share of public monies.

In the Worcester area itself the electioneering campaigns of the five candidates aroused great excitement. The *Worcester Advertiser* of February the 3rd 1894 states:

'At 8 a.m. the contest began, soon thirty or forty carts were plying to and fro, principally those of Joubert and Logan, so much so that one voter went about saying "A voter's life is not a happy one"! And out of a possible 1080 votes, 956 votes were polled.'

On February the 9th the final results were made known. The successful candidate in the entire Worcester constituency was J.D. Logan with 1348 votes. De Villiers had 1092 votes, Meiring 821, Joubert 782 and de Vos 679. Sivewright, as a member of the Afrikaner Bond, must surely have lent a lot of weight to Logan's success, which was quite an achievement for a Progressive in an Afrikaner Bond stronghold!

The final results of the contest were to be announced inside the courtroom when the ballots for all the local polling stations had been collected and counted. However, once Logan knew that he had an unassailable lead, he announced that he had a very pleasant duty to perform, namely, to propose a hearty vote of thanks to Mr. N.P. de Villiers, the Commissioner, for the pleasant and impartial manner in which he had performed the arduous duties of polling officer.

Mr. Logan addressed the electors from the Town Hall balcony as follows. He thanked them very much for placing him at the head of the poll; he felt it was a great honour. He remembered that five years before when he had addressed his electors, the boot had been on the other leg; then he was nearly last. Well, this time he was first in Worcester and stood a good chance of being elected, as he was leading at Matjesfontein, Ceres, Achter Hex River and other key places. He thanked his committee ... and thanked all his electors, English and Dutch, coloured and white, for their loyal support.

He was no 'oprechte Afrikander' but he had made the Colony his home. Some attempt had been made to introduce race-feeling into the political contest but this he strongly deprecated.

He assured them that he intended to fulfil the promises he had made. The bridge and the station they should get, they could depend upon that; if he neglected his duty or failed to give them satisfaction, they might, as soon as opportunity offered, turn him out.

Mr. Logan, on leaving the Town Hall, was caught up by some of his most enthusiastic friends and carried on their shoulders to his carriage. Before you could say "Jack Robinson" the horses were unharnessed and the Laird of Matjesfontein was drawn in triumph to the Masonic Hotel amidst great cheering.

The *Berwickshire Advertiser* in an article published on the 23rd of February 1894, includes a cable sent to J.D. Logan's father Mr James Logan in Scotland from Sir James Sivewright:

'My dear Mr. Logan, it will I am sure be very cheering news to you to know that in the contested election for the representation in our Parliament of Worcester, held yesterday, your son goes in an easy first, has secured a most splendid victory ... Allow me to add my most sincere congratulations to you upon so distinguished an honour being paid to your son and my first friend.

With all good wishes, believe me
Most sincerely yours
J. Sivewright'

The article continues:

'At the last election for the same constituency Mr. Logan was defeated by Mr. J.M.P. de Villiers, and his present majority of 528 votes is ample revenge for the taunt which that gentleman made at the last contest when he reminded his audience that only some fifteen years ago Mr. Logan was a simple railway porter. Mr. Logan's rejoinder on that occasion ... is worth repeating "Yes gentlemen," said Mr. Logan, "fifteen years ago I who am today soliciting the honour of representing you in Parliament, was a simple railway porter, and, as a railway porter I trust I never did a single action, of which, as your representative in Parliament, I or you need feel ashamed; and I am afraid, gentlemen, had the man who has thought it worth his while to make such an accusation against me been, as I was, a railway porter fifteen years ago, he would have been at most a railway porter still." Mr. Logan whose son is at present being educated at Blair Lodge Academy, Stirlingshire intends visiting his native land this summer, when he is sure to meet with an enthusiastic reception by the Restonians in particular, all of whom are justly proud and not a little vain of their illustrious native.'

Jimmy Logan was as good as his word. Shortly after Parliament reassembled he brought a motion for a better station and bridge to be built at Worcester; also, he was most concerned with train safety and questioned whether the Government intended introducing a better system of railway signalling. He quoted instances of gross negligence and inept timetables which could result in two trains arriving at a station at precisely the same time. He concluded by pointing out that there had been 168 railway accidents in the previous three months. In fact the only wonder was that accidents had not occurred with even greater frequency.

One such accident had already claimed the life of John Maitland Grant, a close friend of J.D. Logan's.

Grant was district engineer to the Cape Colony Railways and managed the line from Worcester to Beaufort West. He was accustomed to travelling in his own coach and it was on the fateful day of April the 24th 1891, that his coach was involved in a collision with a railway truck. Grant was killed instantly.

His impressive tomb is to be seen at the little cemetery at Pieter Meintjies. This was a particularly appropriate site for his burial, not only on account of his association with the local railway line, but furthermore because the first few graves there were built for the children of railwaymen who had died during the construction of the line northwards from Touws River. Logan, showing great foresight, had allocated the ground for burial purposes some years before and formalised it as a cemetery when the need for it became apparent.

Logan, as a sheep farmer, was also most concerned with the Scab Act which made it compulsory for farmers to dip their sheep regularly to rid the sheep of this dread disease. The Act was bitterly opposed by farmers who wanted its immediate repeal. Logan realised that the cost of dipping tanks was well beyond the means of many sheep farmers, but advised that negotiations on the ways to implement the Act would be more productive than to call for an Act just passed by Parliament to be repealed, a course of action which could well have the effect of bringing down the Government.

About this time a writer to the *Cape Times* complained of the very bad food offered at some stations 'At some stations the food was almost uneatable and I found this was chiefly at stations managed by a person called Logan – whoever he might be.'

Logan also brought to the notice of the House the curious affair of the water supply to Touws River. Two years earlier, in 1893, Parliament had voted a sum of money for the construction of a reservoir and filter at a railway camp to improve the supply. However, the mandate had been ignored, and day by day, year after year, twenty tons of water had been hauled by rail sixteen miles from the Hex River up a gradient of one-in-forty to ensure a constant water supply for the inhabitants of Touws River. Mr. Laing, the Commissioner, it seems had completely forgotten about the matter until Logan reminded him, and was not aware that water had been hauled up the Hex River Pass for about ten years!

Logan sailed for Scotland in July 1894, leasing Stoneshiel House for the duration of his stay. Interviewed on his arrival overseas as to his political viewpoint he said:

'Well you may say that I am a free lance. I represent, locally, a Dutch constituency, and am glad to say that I enjoy the friendship of Mr. Hofmeyr whom I consider a very sound man indeed... But I am a free lance and provided a measure is good and for the benefit of the common weal I vote for it. If it cannot, I number myself among its most resolute opponents!'

On this trip he visited the South African Students Union Club in Edinburgh, which had been opened the previous year, donating a cheque for one hundred guineas to the Union. This club was a boon and a blessing to the two thousand or more medical students from South Africa whose social life till then had been very bleak. It offered students a library, reading rooms, South African newspapers and a home base.

The *Union Line Gazette* published an article about Matjesfontein on the first of August 1894 that could almost have passed for the Lerner and Loew musical "Camelot"! This read:

'... the temperature is extremely equable. The atmosphere is wonderfully clear and the air is so dry that a gun or rifle may be laid aside uncleaned for an indefinite period after use without the least danger of rusting... the temperature is never oppressingly hot nor unpleasantly cold. In the winter months the hills ... are occasionally snowcapped, and at night light frosts occur frequently, but during the day there is almost invariably warm, bright weather such as entices even extreme invalids out of doors, to their manifest benefit.'

In March 1895 Logan bought the premises of No. 6 Adderley Street for his new wholesale wine and spirit store. These premises were coincidentally almost opposite the old station goods yard where, some sixteen years before, he had first put his foot on the bottom rung of the ladder to fame and fortune.

The following excerpts are taken from a letter written in June 1895 by Robert Craig, an old friend of Logan's. Craig, also formerly of Reston but 'presently' living in East London, South Africa, writes to the *Berwickshire News* of a visit he has just made to Matjesfontein:

'The station at Matjesfontein is one of the finest in South Africa and was created from plans supplied by Mr. Logan ... There are two very handsome dining rooms ... each capable of seating over a hundred guests. These rooms and the whole station in fact are illuminated by electricity and the glass, furniture and plated ware are the best that money can buy.

Attached to the station are spacious lavatories for ladies and gentlemen, and all passenger trains stop here for forty-five minutes for meals ... The village of Matjesfontein lies to the North of the station, the principal buildings consisting of Mr. Logan's beautiful residence, Tweedside Lodge, Schreiner House, where the celebrated authoress of "The Story of an African Farm" lived for three years, and the Masonic Hotel, which are all situated facing the station on a handsome tree-bordered square ... Besides Matjesfontein Mr. Logan owns no less than eleven farms. He thoroughly deserves his success which ... has not been due to lucky speculation in mining shares or to clever money mongering but to foresight, dogged Scottish perseverance, hard thinking and hard work.'

He also refers to Mrs. Logan's being a descendant of one of the oldest Huguenot families, who 'deservedly shares her husband's popularity. Mrs. Logan, indeed, is synonymous with all that is noblest in womanhood and many a consumptive patient who has regained health and hope from the magnificent climate of Matjesfontein bears willing testimony to her thoughtful and unceasing kindness.'

Another visitor at that time also paid tribute to Mrs. Logan. He writes:

'For the time being the Logan colours do not adorn the flagstaff, the Laird being in England, but Mrs. Logan, the most kindly and thoughtful of hostesses, is at home at Tweedside Lodge and dispenses the well-known hospitalities of the house in unostentatious yet liberal spirit. The hostess's goodness and genuine courtesy pervades the whole community and the visitor must be hopeless indeed who is not stimulated and charmed by her happy consideration.'

But the refreshment picture was not always quite so rosy. An irate traveller at Touws River complained bitterly of the quality of the coffee served, to which he was told that the coffee was made according to the practice adopted by the French aristocracy 'who as anybody knows are the only people under the sun who know how to make coffee, and are wise enough to let other folk drink it!'

The unhappy traveller went on to say:

'On a recent occasion a number of gentlemen were compelled to go without their dinner at Springfontein owing to the poor quality of the fare provided. I was one of the number and as we had all prepaid the guard under the new arrangement we were precluded from any redress.'

This traveller was to conclude in a letter to the *Cape Times* that 'it is high time that the Railway Department insisted on a thorough reform on the part of the refreshment room contractor!'

Matjesfontein remained Logan's pride and joy, hardly to be forgotten among all his other business and his political life. He steadily continued to improve the village and in January 1896 the opening ceremony of the new building to be used as both a school and a concert hall, took place. Colonel Frederick Xavier Schermbrucker gave the opening address, which was followed by a concert and supper. Later that year the inspector of schools, Mr. J.R. Cuthbert, visited Matjesfontein and was 'surprised and delighted with the handsome and roomy building.'

He is reported to have said at the time:

'Very few towns in South Africa can boast such excellent school accommodation, certainly no village in this part of the world can show anything to compare with it!'

At a meeting of the Board at Ceres in April 1896 the Honourable P.B. van Rhyn, Member of the Legislative Council, raised, among other contentious issues, the question of Sunday travelling. A resolution had been passed condemning the practice of morning trains on Sunday; it being considered wrong that the Sabbath should be used for travelling. However, a select committee appointed by Parliament had subsequently reported that it would be impossible to put a stop to this practice.

Mr. Logan expressed himself as sympathising greatly with the feelings of those so vehement on the matter on account of their religious principles, but at the same time confessed that he could not think of supporting such a motion. They might as well try to stop the tide ebbing and flowing by legislation, as do this. Take, for example, the train which passed through Matjesfontein on Saturday night and reached Triangle, one of the loneliest spots in the district, at about 11.30 on the same night. According to such a resolution, the train would then have to remain there until twelve o' clock the following night!

What a pleasant time the passengers would have of it, what with the excellent opportunity it would afford for activities such as drinking and card-playing, which were in themselves infinitely worse than mere travelling. On the other hand, if the train were allowed to proceed in the usual way, all or most of these people would be home in time to go to church if they so wished. He was sorry but it was absolutely impossible for him ever to agree with them on this point. (Hear, Hear and Cheers!)

Logan also expressed a keen interest in the language issues of the day. At a meeting of the Ceres branch of the Dutch Bond in May 1896, the chairman brought a motion that it was necessary for everyone holding any public position to be capable of conversing in Dutch as well as English. Mr. Logan was of the opinion that everyone should know the language of the country in which they dwelt. Personally he knew enough Dutch to carry him along in the ordinary way but he was hardly sufficiently well up in it to attempt to use it in making a speech.

Meanwhile Logan's business affairs had grown to such an extent that in June he floated his own company, James D. Logan and Company Limited. The company aimed to carry on the business of merchandising and dealing in wine and spirits, to contract for and keep refreshment rooms, bars and hotels and much more besides. All this activity was to be directed from No. 6 Adderley Street, which Logan had enlarged and improved. He also mooted plans to erect another four-storey building behind and facing onto St. George's Street. The *Argus* commented that:

'... this would mean one more step towards making St. George's Street the second-finest thoroughfare in Cape Town.'

Logan also bought a farm called "de Draai" at Touws River later in the year.

The "Reformers" who had been arrested and held in custody in January 1896 after the abortive Jameson Raid, were released in June and sent to Cape Town en route to England. Logan, on being approached to attach a dining car to the train in which the "Reformers" were travelling, immediately put a dining car at their disposal with only one stipulation – that the travellers should be his guests from Johannesburg to Cape Town. However, should anyone of the party offer to pay for anything, this generous offer would fall away!

Before their ship sailed these travellers invited Logan on board to present him with a magnificent silver tea and coffee service and salver inscribed

'Presented to J.D. Logan Esq., Member of the Legislative Assembly, as a token of appreciation on behalf of his guests in the special "Reform" train from Johannesburg to Cape Town. June 1896.'

Legend has it that a small group of "Reformers" fled Johannesburg and hid in the hills behind Tweedside. Jimmy Logan is reputed to have driven by Cape Cart from Matjesfontein to Tweedside once a week for about three weeks, bearing a case of whisky which he would conceal at a prearranged spot near the farmhouse, to quench the thirst of the escapees! Four of the "Reformers" were supposedly hidden in the cellars underneath the station building at Matjesfontein for some time, only daring to venture out from their sanctuary at nightfall.

A pair of elaborately decorated Chinese vases, now in John Buist's possession, bear mute witness to this curious, heroic episode in Matjesfontein's history. These were dedicated to Emma Logan by the fugitives, the inscription conveying their grateful thanks to her for the kindness and care she showed them while they were in hiding. Meanwhile, in terms of the ongoing affairs of state, the railways and irrigation schemes continued to dominate matters debated in the House while the controversial Scab Act, passed some two years before, still troubled some of the members.

In Parliament Jimmy Logan had shown himself to be a very dedicated and hard-working representative. He would ask his constituents to let him know in advance of matters causing them concern so that he could present their case in the best possible terms in every instance. He showed an independent grasp of a wide range of subjects in general terms, subjects such as education, farming and the railways. He also demonstrated, more specifically, a very detailed knowledge in the matter of the Touws River water supply and an equally acute knowledge of the Scab Act. Further, as mentioned above, Logan would on many occasions raise the very vexed question of railway signalling, such was his concern with public safety and comfort and his preoccupation with efficiency and progress.

As a result of the Jameson Raid, Cecil John Rhodes tendered his resignation as Prime Minister and was summoned to England to testify before a parliamentary committee investigating the Raid. While Rhodes was overseas many of his former friends and fellow parliamentarians turned against him. The whole affair was hotly debated in the Cape Parliament in May 1896. Jimmy Logan was very strongly of the opinion that it was premature and unworthy of others to judge Rhodes' actions before the outcome of his trial was known. Further, he, Logan, had always adhered to the view that it was one of the highest traditions of the British nation never to kick a man when he was down, or attack anyone in his absence, when he was unable to put his case and defend himself.

The majority in Parliament deplored the Raid but nevertheless conceded that the so-called "Uitlanders", or newly-arrived immigrant workers in South Africa, had definite and long-standing grievances which they had tried repeatedly but in vain to have redressed.

Contrarily, Olive Schreiner let it be known that not one of her three brothers living on the Rand had ever written to her that he was dissatisfied with his treatment by the Boers or that he was anxious to obtain civil rights!

Tweedside Lodge at Matjiesfontein

CHAPTER IX

JUBILEE YEAR

The eagerly-awaited new Worcester bridge was formally opened in January 1897 by Mrs. Meiring, wife of the mayor of Worcester, who baptised it with the traditional bottle of champagne. Sir James Sivewright in his address thanked the members of Parliament Messrs. de Villiers and Logan for all the work they had done in promoting and facilitating the building of the bridge.

In June of that year Logan again brought to the attention of the House the urgent need for a new railway station at Worcester. He reminded the members that this need had been recognised by the Commissioner of Railways some three years before. A start on the project had indeed been made; one new platform and some minor alterations, supposedly the nucleus of the new station, were by now complete. However, since then he had repeatedly approached the Government for further action, but the new Worcester station was still 'conspicuous by its absence!'

Sir James Sivewright replied that plans were under way, and when the station yard extensions and road works were completed, construction would begin.

Indeed 1897, which had begun so propitiously with the opening of the new bridge at Worcester, was a very productive year all round for J. D. Logan. In March of that year he purchased the Royal Hotel in Hout Bay for twelve thousand pounds and just three months later, in June 1897, the African Banking Corporation opened a branch at Matjesfontein. We are told that this handsome building, put up by Logan, was completed in only seven weeks! There was a large gathering present when Logan unlocked the doors of the new bank and formally welcomed the manager, Mr. R. F. Aling, who replied briefly. The bank immediately commenced business, 'a large sum of money being paid in forthwith!' A luncheon followed, with toasts and speeches. Logan referred to the political situation and to an attempt which had been made the previous evening to upset the Government.

His feelings in the present case were, that it was clearly a case of rather 'let them prefer the devil they knew to the devil they knew too well!'

And to round off the celebrations? We read that 'an interesting game of cricket of which the destructive nature of the Laird's bowling was the feature, brought the proceedings to a close.'

This event was reported in the *Cape Times.* A few days later a letter appeared in the same newspaper under the title 'Advance Laingsburg', expressing these sentiments:

' ... Laingsburg versus Matjesfontein and Touws River. The first is a progressing village, going ahead, not in "Talk of the Day" but in reality ... While our antagonistic neighbour brags of banks and doctors, we are building large substantial dwelling houses, produce stores, etc. We have three butchers and send meat to the city. One week we see a fine billiard table at Mr. Horne's commodious hotel, the next an additional bobby patrols our streets. Now again a Village Board! A private farm "be its owner ever so great' cannot cross swords with us!" CORRESPONDENT.

Queen Victoria's Golden Jubilee on June the 25th was celebrated all over the British Empire, not least at Matjesfontein, where the entire village was en fête. The station and Logan's house were ablaze with flags and bunting. A luncheon was followed by sports on the big square behind the station. Races, tugs-of-war, jumping and other competitions were held, in which children of all races took part. At three o'clock the school children, bearing flags and banners, walked to the little school house which had been completed in 1896, where they were presented with beautiful Jubilee mugs which today are greatly treasured by those lucky enough to have inherited or acquired them; prizes were handed out, the National Anthem sung, and in the evening there was a fireworks display!

Another of the concerts for which Matjesfontein was by now quite famous ensued, and this was followed by a dance which effectively brought the Jubilee Festivities to a close. There were all kinds of performances during the celebration, including recitations, duets and comic solos, as well as songs sad and humorous. One can but speculate on the nature and talents of a certain Miss Nettle, who obliged with a pianoforte solo; wonder about a Mr. and Mrs. Monday, a Mr. T. Begbie and a Mr. M. Maxwell, who all sang at the concert. All we do know is that the encores were numerous. Many of these persons were mentioned in other concerts.

On this particular evening the concert was followed by a play. There were votes of thanks to the chairman, Dr. Robertson, three cheers for Mr. and Mrs. Logan and the singing of "God Save the Queen". Then a dance ensued, to be kept up 'till the wee sma' hours a yint the twal!' or until the arrival of the morning train by which most of the Touws River contingent departed. What an enchanting picture is conjured up of a bygone age!

Around this time Logan offered to give Touws River a recreation ground and fifty pounds towards laying it out. One reaction to this offer in a letter to the Midland News was that it would be more valuable for Logan to provide decent coffee at Touws River 'as the abominable mixture served out at present is a constant source of complaint!'

The *Cape Times*, referring to the lack of sports amenities at Touws River, commented that it was 'disgraceful that the oldest railway camp in the Colony had no club for games or sports, the billiard table at the Railway Institute presenting the sole remaining means of recreation. It is true that a lawn tennis club exists but this is confined to the officials ... At best lawn tennis is but a young-ladyish sort of pastime, and no substitute for the manly games, cricket and football which, on the authority of a great general, have laid the foundations for so many victories, afloat and ashore!'

Many instances of Jimmy Logan's generosity are recorded; among them, various donations including fifty guineas to the new sports ground at Worcester, lamps for the new buildings for the pupils of the Deaf, Dumb and Blind Institute at Worcester, a silver cup presented to the Berwick-on-Tweed Volunteer Rifles, two hundred pounds towards a Sailors and Soldiers Clubhouse in Cape Town, while back in Touws River he donated ground for a church for the Coloured community.

That winter in Matjesfontein a football club was

formed, calling itself the Matjesfontein Logandas! And to promote sport of another kind Logan supervised the placing of five thousand trout into the Hex River for the enjoyment of anglers. On the 5th of November 1897 the opening of the railway line to Bulawayo by the Governor of the Cape Colony, Sir Alfred Milner, was celebrated in grand style. Two special trains from Cape Town carried invited guests, among whom were many members of the Legislative Assembly, including Logan himself.

This event was heralded, in the words of the High Commissioner as 'an important day in the history of South Africa and the Empire.' And in an editorial the *Argus* remarks 'The Bulawayo railway is one of the magnificent amends Mr. Rhodes is making for the mistakes of the past.'

Logan had of course been responsible for the railway catering on these trains and on this occasion passengers were unanimous in agreeing that their creature comforts had been well catered for, so much so that a complimentary address was presented to Logan.

In a letter to the press at this time VIATOR writes:

'As an old traveller I should like to say that the meals served at C. G. R. Refreshment Rooms leave little to be desired ... Your correspondents who find fault with the refreshment rooms on the Cape Government Railways should try a trip over the Natal or Free State lines. If they turn up their noses at the meals on our railway, I wonder what they would do in the case of either of the latter ... For myself I know a good meal when I see it, and I think anyone who finds fault with the food at the refreshment stations on Cape

Railways is either a hypercritical hypochondriac or a glutton...'

But a correspondent to the *Standard and Diggers News* had a very different opinion:

' ... the unfortunate Johannesburger who travels to and from the Cape is exasperated beyond measure at bad and ill-cooked food served at extortionate prices and by insolent attendants who crush you if you dare make mild protest. If Mr. Logan does not take care there will be a big outcry against the monopoly and the extension of it to Bulawayo.'!

The old School House built in 1896

Chinese vases presented to J.D. Logan

CHAPTER X

J.D. LOGAN IS ELECTED TO THE LEGISLATIVE COUNCIL

Towards the end of 1897 and perhaps at Rhodes' urging, Logan decided he would stand for election to the Higher House in the North Western Constituency. Accordingly he resigned from the Lower House and offered himself as a candidate for the Higher House in the election which took place on the 16th of March 1898. The *Worcester Standard* commented thus in an editorial in March 1898:

'... The Cape is emphatically the country of the moderate man ... It is the man of sound moderate opinions ... who is progressive in all those matters that make for the welfare of the land ...Worcester is happy in having had its necessities recognized in such a handsome manner ... Mr Logan may be safely looked to, to see that even-handed justice is meted out. He has lived in the Karoo for twenty years and should, therefore, be well-acquainted with our requirements. What we want is not a man who will be content to represent us merely for three months in the year when Parliament is in session, during which the money-grabbing members principally look forward to their handsome allowance of one pound sixteen shillings per day, but one who will keep a watchful eye upon our interests all the year round.

'... He has done this successfully on behalf of the division of Worcester and that is the guarantee that he will do his best for the larger area he now seeks to represent.'

And much more, ending with the stirring words, 'If then, they (the electors of the North Western Circle) are the men we take them for, they will see to it that Mr Logan is returned at the head of the poll.'

The *Cape Times* of March the 9th 1898 mentions that 'Mr. J. D. Logan, M. L. A., has purchased the *Worcester Standard* from Mr. F. Lindenburg, the former proprietor.'

However, despite the many glowing tributes dedicated to Logan and the confidence he seemed to inspire in others, sentiments about him were by no means unanimous. In particular, the candidatures of both J. D. Logan and Anders Ohlson, Consul-General for Sweden, were singled out for severe criticism in an aggressive attack.

A strong opinion was voiced that these two were only standing in an attempt to gain further power and influence, whereby they would find themselves in a position, *inter alia,* to circumvent the highly contentious Liquor Law Amendment Bill. This was a bill designed to force some restriction on the sale of liquor, which would of course be detrimental to liquor sales in Logan's refreshments rooms and sales of Ohlson's 'tickey beer', a popular local drink favoured especially by the more indigent inhabitants of the Cape Colony!

The North Western Circle consisted of the Parliamentary districts of Worcester, Malmesbury, Piquetburg, Namaqualand and Clanwilliam. Opposing Logan, the Progressive candidate in this election, were, respectively: Van Rhyn, Lochner and Rabie, all

Afrikaner Bond; and 'Joubert, Independent. Van Rhyn took great exception to Mr. C.A. Pilkington's sending printed circulars to voters in Namaqualand inviting them to vote for Logan. He wrote to Pilkington:

'I have heard you had sent printed circulars and letters ... containing your kind request and stating "If you wish anything done for Namaqualand go and plump for Mr. Logan". I invite you to attend a public meeting at Mesklip at which I intend addressing the meeting. I trust you are a man of courage and not a coward ... Therefore I again invite and challenge you to meet me at the meeting. You will then be placed in the opportunity to state publicly and not on the sly, what your candidate has already done ... and to describe his virtue, honesty, dignity, and usefulness, etc.'

To which Pilkington replied:

'I am only too glad to find my circulars have had the desired effect upon your "nest". You write that you hear I have sent out circulars. Yes, about six hundred and I am sending two copies for your edification, one in the "taal" and one in English. I would send more for distribution but have none left ... Take my advice, put your tail between your legs and come no further as you will not get a single vote at Springbok, O'Kiep, Concordia, Steinhopf or Port Nolloth. I should very much like to see you face Mr. Logan on a platform and I'm sure he would be delighted to meet you ...!'

He adds further 'You wrote me where Mesklip is. I saw it before you ever knew there was such a place!'

At the close of polling at Worcester, a Mr. Olive thanked voters on behalf of Mr. Logan 'because he was away looking after places he could not trust so well as

Worcester!' A report from O'Kiep stated that polling was vigorous and that Logan's chances were high. The North Western Circle results were published on March the 23rd, and as the *Cape Times* put it, 'Mr. J. D. Logan, Progressive, has simply romped in'. His majority over his nearest rival, Mr. P.B. Van Rhyn of the Bond, was a substantial 3762.

In the final results Logan polled 7375 votes and Van Rhyn 3613.

Mr. Van Rhyn did not take his defeat lightly! This translation of his letter to the Dutch Press was published in the *Cape Times* on April the 6th 1896:

'Mr. P. B. Van Rhyn contributes a letter to "Ons Land". He is immensely proud that he has been returned at the bottom of the poll, for he argues that one of his supporters being any day worth three of Mr. Logan's, he virtually stands at the head of the poll. He scorns the idea of being returned to Parliament by men of Logan's supporters' stamp. At the same time he is determined to be revenged upon the coloured people of the mission stations, and forthwith appeals to all the members of the Dutch Reformed Church not to contribute to the Colonial Missions Fund until such time as the mission stations have been deprived of the franchise. Ex-elder at the church though he be, he does not hesitate to call the mission-stations a curse.'

On March the 24th the *Cape Times* commented on Logan's election, 'Mr. Logan's achievement at being placed at head of the poll being brought about because although he (Logan) has made no promises and goes to the council absolutely untrammelled, all classes of the community have faith in his honesty, sound common sense and business ability that he has been returned at the head of the poll by such a splendid majority.'

Soon after the election a traveller, the Rev. Lionel Bamford, wrote to the *Berwickshire News* that, 'having passed through the abomination of desolation he found himself in a veritable Garden of Eden at Matjesfontein.'

It was even more to his surprise when the train stopped there for the travellers to have breakfast, that the very first man he should meet should be a Scotsman, an old man dressed in coarse workman's clothes, who turned out to be J. D. Logan's father on a visit to his son! The two became fast friends, finding they lived only six miles apart and had many mutual friends. He relates with some affection his welcome in Matjesfontein, saying, 'the kindly old man rightly guesses that I must be somewhat tired and dusty after the all-night journey, and takes me to a splendid big swimming pond, fitted with dressing boxes, where one has a delightfully refreshing swim, and dress in time to resume one's journey!'

The Owl Club, founded in 1894, numbered Logan among its members. At a meeting of the club at the end of May 1898 at Poole's Hotel in Cape Town, Private Edgar Wallace, one of the invited guests, entertained the company with an original recitation of the patriotic song "In the presence of the Queen". Many musical items followed, and at midnight Jimmy Logan took over the chair from a Mr. Tennyson Cole, immediately asking the gentlemen present to be his guests and to drink to the health of Her Most Gracious Majesty.

This was done in bumpers of champagne, remarking the fact that nowhere in the British Empire would Her Majesty's Birthday be honoured more punctually than by the Owls and their friends!

Jimmy Logan junior, a keen sportsman, was to win the public school championship for bowling in Scotland before suffering a badly broken arm in a rugby match. The arm had to be reset, and notwithstanding his recent election to the Legislative Council, J. D. Logan decided that he must travel to Scotland with his wife Emma to visit Jimmy. Accordingly the Logans sailed for Britain on board H.R.M.S. *Norman.* They once more leased Netherbyres House in Scotland, where they, as was their custom, entertained many friends both old and new. Asked in an interview about his political career Logan replied 'I took to the forum like a duck to water'. He was known as a staunch supporter of Rhodes, a logical debater and an authority on railways.

Arthur Shed, who remembered Logan as a boy, also recalled two of his brothers visiting Logan, perhaps at Stoneshiel or Netherbyres, and returning home having imbibed not wisely but too well!

The Logans entertained generously at Netherbyres. On one occasion Logan planned a treat for the schoolchildren. Led by a piper, they marched to a large field where after a hearty lunch, contests of skill and strength and various games and sports took place; prizes were awarded, an ample tea was arranged and there were yet more games and sports, the day ending with some dancing and hearty cheers for the donor of the feast. The Logans returned to South Africa in October, bringing their son with them. We read that when their train pulled out of Reston station 'the Laird and his party left behind them a platform packed with county friends and villagers to bid them a hearty good-bye, and as hearty a welcome back again.

William Dabbs' Steam Engine at Cape Town Station

CHAPTER XI

DISASTER

While the Logans were overseas one of the most tragic railway accidents in South African history took place near Matjesfontein. This accident stunned the country. Not only did it shock and horrified the entire nation, but its effects reverberated around the world. Brokers and speculators alike, many of whom had friends and relatives who had hurried across the sea to the Eldorado in the plains of Africa, to the newly-discovered goldfields deep in the folds of the Witwatersrand, panicked at the news. The official accounts of the disaster led to an alarm which spread all the way from a chaotic Johannesburg, across the waves to London and beyond.

Emma and her daughter Gertrude were in London when the crash occurred and saw the headlines "Train disaster at Matjesfontein" in a London paper.

The accident moreover could have been predicted, such were its circumstances. From Matjesfontein the original line ran towards the interior over a high neck of solid rock near a small station named Mostert's Hoek. Banking engines were kept at Laingsburg to help southbound trains to negotiate the steep neck.

This potentially perilous maneouvre was indeed to have a tragic sequel when on the 16th of August 1898 a runaway truck from Mostert's Hoek crashed into a southbound train pulling out of Laingsburg.

Ironically, the chief of the Railways economic department, by name Mr. H. M. Beatty, was a passenger in the train at the time. His report, wired from Matjesfontein, made chilling reading to friends and relatives in London:

'I was a passenger in 4-up today, Tuesday. The train consisted of two engines and seven bogie vehicles.' About six miles south of Laingsburg we came into collision with the runaway portion of the 48 train up which was travelling at a high rate of speed. The 'leading engine of 4-up mounted the trucks. The second engine kept the rails with the exception of the leading bogie. The wheels of the T P O van behind the second engine telescoped into the Netherlands Coach, the first three compartments of which were completely wrecked.'

Two men, one woman and a child travelling in the Netherlands coach were killed ... Driver O'Brien of the first engine is suffering from internal injury. The driver and fireman of the second engine were not injured. Several natives who were travelling in the runaway portion of the 48 - up are killed or injured. The remaining portion of the train caught fire but fortunately did not explode ... The rear portion of the 48 - up ran away at Mostert's Hoek siding.'

Further information from Matjesfontein states:

' ... the sight that met the eye on arrival was awful. The front part of the train was smashed to matchwood and together with wood from the trucks was blazing like a huge bonfire. It is said that at least ten of the natives who were in the front truck were literally burnt to death, their injuries prevented them from moving from the mass of burning wood ... On the left side of the train were lying four or five corpses of natives and several boys who had been badly injured. Five

Europeans have been killed, the Rev. and Mrs. du Toit and a little girl of Dewetsdorp, and Mr. de Villiers senior and Davie Cope, the Johannesburg football player, on his way to join the Currie Cup tournament. In the same carriage, the first, with Cope, were Mr. J. Rees of East London and Tait another football player, who were both badly injured ...'

Some headlines in the daily newspapers paint a vivid picture: "Tidings of Cope's death casts a gloom over the town"; "Consternation in the Golden City"; "15 Natives burnt to death"; "Football match postponed". And sadly "How poor Davie lost his life"; "Harrowing scenes."

Yet more press reports state that owing to the death of Mr. Cope, 'the match Transvaal and Eastern Province has been postponed' and later, 'The Transvaal team has promised to continue the tournament after tomorrow out of consideration for the other visiting teams. The Transvaal team will wear some symbol of mourning on the arm in their match against Rhodesia on Saturday.'

Another journalist describes the carnage and confusion around the scene of the accident in graphic detail:

'Cope was simply crushed to death, his body being squeezed fiat in a most horrible manner ... His body was lying above Rees when the latter was extricated from the wreckage. A Post Office official in the Travelling Post Office was in the top bunk when the accident happened and though the carriage was telescoped he escaped without hurt. He was pulled naked through the roof by friendly hands'.

Tait, interviewed at the hospital, says he was

talking to Mr. Rees the well-known Border halfback with Cope seated opposite him, when suddenly they experienced a terrific shock. He was conscious of a feeling of being lifted from his seat and then a body was literally propelled at him. It struck the upper berth, then fell on his chest, pinning him where he was. He must have lapsed into a state of insensibility. Afterwards he heard the rescuers trying to make their way to the bodies. After waiting a long time he heard one man say that it was impossible to do more.

Davie Cope was regarded as 'about the best full-back in Rugby football on the Rand.'

In one obituary a sportswriter "The Mug" wrote:

'Cope was one of those cool, calm and cautious players ... and his fame as a safe tackler and an excellent punter will live in the minds of those who follow South African Rugby football for many a long year to come ... As a full back he was up to the end one of the finest South Africa has yet produced, making others pale into insignificance. Poor Davie! Requiescat in Pace.'

Soon after these tragic events the railway line was re-routed to its present position. Shortly afterwards the new Laingsburg station was built.

The Lord Milner Hotel shortly after the cessation of hostilities in the Anglo-Boer War

The present-day Lord Milner Hotel, only the flag has changed

CHAPTER XII

THE GREAT NEWSPAPER DEBATE AND MURRAY BISSET'S CRICKET XI

Railways and irrigation were the main subjects debated in the House throughout 1898, while the Scab Act, passed some two years before, continued to trouble some members.

On one occasion, Jimmy Logan and W.P. Schreiner came into open confrontation in the house when Logan was moved to describe a particular action on Schreiner's part as obstruction. He said he had not come to play marbles but to do business.

Schreiner retorted that Logan always opposed everything proposed by anybody else, manifesting a sudden interest in the bill before the committee when he came in, though he did not always seem to know what side of the house he was on!

Apart from the catering contract another Logan contract that caused great controversy was that which was drawn up between the Government and J.D. Logan and Co., awarding the latter the sole right to sell newspapers at railway stations. This contract, drawn up some three years previously, was not immediately implemented, but in March 1899 a deputation of station masters brought their grievances to the Commissioner of Railways, Mr. J.W. Sauer. They had just been notified that J.D. Logan and Co. were about to exercise their right to set up bookstalls and sell newspapers at suburban stations, and that the station masters must cease their sales of newspapers. For many years station masters had been able to sell newspapers on their stations, which had brought in a welcome addition to their salaries. Of course, the general public aligned themselves on one side or the other; some questioned the legalities of the contract and bemoaned the lot of the poor station master; others opined that the station masters were well-paid and as public servants were not permitted to engage in other business or trade.

But the overriding point at issue seemed to be that the contract had been altered since being approved by the Tender Board in that (a) Logan's contract was subject to twelve and not six months notice, and (b) the station masters' privileges which had been preserved, had subsequently been removed.

Accordingly, in July Mr. J. T. Molteno brought the affair before the House and moved for a return of all existing contracts relating to the sale of newspapers upon the Cape Government Railways, as well as all other pertinent correspondence and papers. The upshot being, that after a great deal of debate and insinuation, it was recommended that the contract should be terminated as soon as was legally possible. Further, it was recommended that the station masters involved should be recompensed for any losses they might have sustained. The whole incident made clear that, in principle, members of Parliament should not be permitted to tender for government contracts. This was the law in England, law which, it was hoped, would soon apply in South Africa.

Logan was however in the meantime awarded the refreshment contract from Vryburg to Bulawayo in May of 1899, which must have been a consolation to him for the loss of sole newspaper rights on the railway stations.

A touring South African cricket team calling themselves the "Bashi-Bazouks" and captained by Murray Bisset, visited Matjiesfontein in September 1899 for a friendly match – which indeed turned out to be a *very*' friendly match, for the visitors allowed the home team to field no less than eighteen players! In an 'after match' speech Murray Bissett said of Logan:

'No man has done more for cricket in South Africa than Mr. Logan. We know it was he who initiated the visits of Lord Hawke's teams to this country, which has done so much for cricket. A gentleman now high up in the political arena once said he wished there were ten thousand Logans (John X. Merriman) ... and I am sure we all wish there were ten thousand Logans.'

Logan replied:

'... I look to the good old English game of cricket to do much towards uniting the different classes in this country... and it is my ambition that the day will come when a team will go to England as good as they can send from Australia.'

Water was, as always, at a premium in South Africa. Late in 1898 the government began boring for water near the station at Matjesfontein and in spite of dire predictions of failure – 'there is as much possibility of finding water at Matjesfontein as there is of finding green cheese on the moon' was one opinion – subterranean water was found in great quantities, and a steam pump brought up water at the rate of twenty-three thousand gallons a day. Geological surveys took place at roughly the same time and these gave indication of promising coal deposits in the Karoo.

Logan celebrated his 41st birthday on November the 26th with a party for fifty friends and employees. As was the custom on such occasions, the day was declared a holiday and observed as such. It began with a cricket match, followed by a lavish meal complete with bumpers of champagne – then tennis and socialising until the light failed. Jimmy's old friend Colonel Schermbrucker attended the festivities and proposed a toast to the Laird's health.

Around the time of his birthday celebrations, Logan quite appropriately added Belmont House at Ceres to his already impressive list of properties, a birthday present to himself perhaps, as well as a boon to the villagers of Ceres!

The British encampment outside Matjesfontein before the battle of Magersfontein

The Olive Schreiner Cottage

CHAPTER XIII

WAR CLOUDS

Coming events, they say, cast their shadows before. Military field operations had already taken place in Natal. Now, at the end of 1898, as the cape Colony prepared to launch a series of military manoeuvres, the Western Province would be divided into two states, the two capitals being Cape Town and Matjesfontein, bordered by the Winterhoek Mountains and the Breede River. For nearly a week the troops, consisting on the one side of the Kings Royal Rifles and Mounted Infantry, and on the other the 1st Liverpool Regiment, carried out a series of mock engagements. The premise was that diplomatic relations having been broken off, the General Officer Commanding the Eastern Forces had crossed the frontier with hostile intent. (It is to be noted with some relief, that only blank cartridges were used!) Stringent orders were issued regarding the crossing of standing crops and generally respecting the wishes all property owners concerned. The Royal Army Medical Corps also took part in the exercise.

While the Colony interested itself mainly in railways, newspaper contracts, water boring, geological exploration, sports, entertainment, wine production and the price of mutton, events to the north were reaching critical proportions.

The discovery of gold and before that diamonds had forever changed the future of the South African Republic, the future of the Cape Colony and indeed, the fixture of the whole of Southern Africa. Gold, the capricious noble metal which had succeeded in casting its spell over mankind for thousands of years, suddenly appeared in vast quantities to dominate local politics and economics, holding the entire local populace in its thrall. The Afrikaner stronghold across the Vaal River was found to be the site of probably the largest gold deposits ever discovered. In the face of a huge and ever-increasing influx of gold diggers, fortune hunters, entrepreneurs, engineers and other assorted immigrants, Paul Kruger, president of the Republic, tried to stem the tide in order to maintain the agricultural, pastoral, cultural and religious life style he and his fellow trekkers had sought in great adversity to establish. He and his fellow Afrikaners felt that they had to preserve their separate identity and retain their independence in the face of this invasion of foreigners. The spectre of British domination in particular was very real to them.

Alfred Lord Milner, Governor of the Cape Colony since 1897, and before that chairman of the Board of Inland Revenue in Britain for five years, was well aware of how important gold was to Britain. The metal was of prime significance and large reserves were needed by the Exchequer to underpin sterling and maintain the entire British economy. Further, gold in sufficient quantities would ensure that London would remain the centre of world finance. However, Britain's gold reserves were running low, while gold in enormous quantities lay just over the borders of the Cape Colony, tantalisingly out of reach of His Majesty's government. The annexation of the Transvaal would seem to provide the perfect solution to the problem. Further, there was a legitimate pretext for the interference by His Majesty's government in the affairs of the fledgling Boer Republic - the grievances of the so-called "Uitlanders" in the Transvaal. It was they who would provide the initial justification and the eventual leverage, to bring about the forced inclusion of the Boer Republic into the sprawling British Empire. The "Uitlanders" main grievance was essentially the severe and lengthy terms and conditions that were imposed on them before they were granted the franchise. In many instances they found themselves paying most of the local taxes without being afforded any real voting rights or effective representation.

The Jameson Raid in 1895 only succeeded in exacerbating already strained relations between the Boers and the British (Joseph Chamberlain, Britain's Colonial Secretary was certainly aware of the planning of the Raid). Although after the Raid Kruger had made certain concessions to the "Uitlanders", these were perceived not to be enough, and the "Uitlanders" appealed to the British Government for help. Milner ended one telegram to Chamberlain by asserting 'the case for intervention is overwhelming'.

In June another company of the Army Service Corps was readied for the Cape. Soon thereafter H.M.S. *Powerful* arrived in Durban, sailing for Cape Town on October the 11th.

Milner felt that a strong show of force was needed for Kruger to accede to the British demands and in a further cable to Chamberlain he wrote 'with an army actually on their borders they will submit to anything and everything...'

However, when British troops began to assemble

on the borders of the Transvaal, Paul Kruger sent his own demand - an ultimatum that the troops be withdrawn.

This ultimatum expired at 5 p.m. on October the 11th, 1899 (the day after Paul Kruger's birthday, coincidentally), leaving Britain officially at war with the South African Republic.

The international *Bankers Magazine* for November 1899 noted that 'the leading monetary power in the world' was at war with 'a country producing the greater proportion of the world's supply of gold.'

The Anglo-Boer War which began in 1899 has been described not only as 'the last of the gentleman's wars', but as one of the saddest conflicts in South African history. This was perhaps because the spectacle of the most powerful nation on earth engaged in bloody conflict with a small, vastly outnumbered army of Boer farmers, fighting not only for all that they held dear, but their very lives and the lives of those around them, was enough to capture the sympathetic interest of the world.

Indeed, the bloodstained, sunburnt battlefields of the South African veldt where the hardy, resourceful Boer could be seen to clash head-on with the might of the British war machine, became a focus for world attention, fascinating but sickening countless onlookers.

These were turbulent times and when war came, the Laird was ready. He raised and commanded a troop of one hundred men, called the Matjesfontein Mounted Rifles. Awarded the rank of major by the Imperial War Office, J. D. Logan proceeded to play an important part in the battles of Belmont and Modder River as well as participating in a number of other military engagements, having his horse shot from under him on one occasion. He later received two medals with clasps for bravery, being mentioned in despatches for the part he played in the war.

It was the Anglo-Boer War that brought the great British commanders of the age to South Africa, who counted among their number Lord Roberts, Douglas Haig - later to become the Field Marshal of Flanders fame - and Lord Ironside, who commanded a field battery of the Royal Artillery at Matjesfontein.

Ironside was later, in 1940, to become British Chief of Imperial General Staff.

At one time Lord Ironside, in company with Douglas Haig, was billeted in J.D. Logan's private house. Ironside, a brilliant linguist, was said to have had a working knowledge of eighteen languages. He reputedly learnt what was then called "Cape Dutch", the forerunner of Afrikaans, in his rare moments of spare time whilst staying at Matjesfontein.

It was events leading up to the Boer War too, that brought an unknown soldier by the name of Edgar Wallace to the shores of Africa, before he was to achieve fame and fortune as a writer of successful thrillers.

What did they think of the tiny village of Matjesfontein as the train clanked on against a background as ancient as time itself? One soldier is on record as referring to his surroundings as 'this infernal Karoo'.

Matjesfontein played host to many famous regiments, both from Cape Town and overseas. These included the Coldstream Guards, the 17th Lancers, the

Middlesex Regiment and the Duke of Edinburgh's Own Rifles. Troops in transit camped around the village and thronged the main street in khaki uniforms and service boots.

At the remount station across the railway line, the young, high-spirited Gertrude Logan would often help the troops exercise their horses in the Karoo she knew so well.

There was no actual fighting in the Matjesfontein area although a few shots were exchanged with roving Hoer Commandos from time to time.

However, not far away from the village, at the farm then known as "Karbonaatjies Kraal", a young Jan Christiaan Smuts on commando with the Boer troops was able to elude the British forces by escaping up the kloof escarpment behind the farm.

On November the 24th 1899 a Mrs. Hanbury Williams wrote to the Honourable J.D. Logan from Government House, Cape Town:

> **'Dear Sir,**
>
> **I am engaged with others here in carrying out Red Cross work for the benefit of sick and wounded in the present war.**
>
> **It is desired to form a connection with the head centre in Cape Town, which embraces the Good Hope Society, the St. John Ambulance Associations and the British Red Cross Society. Agencies at the places on the Railway, through which the sick and wounded will pass from the front to the base hospitals at Wynberg, or who may be detained as patients in hospital - with a view to affording them comforts at such places.**

It is essential however, that such aid should be rendered only under arrangements approved by the local Military Medical Authorities and as a branch of the Red Cross work organised there.

I should be glad therefore to receive the names of a small number of ladies and gentlemen say not exceeding 6, who would form themselves into a local Red Cross Committee, who will work in aid of the sick and wounded under the above conditions, and who will act as correspondents for the Head Centre, and as an Agent for receiving and distributing stores sent up from here.

An early answer would be much appreciated.

I am yours faithfully

Annie G. Hanbury Williams.'

The Hotel Milner was temporarily the headquarters of the Cape Command and became for a short while a convalescent home for officers.

On November the 28th 1899 Logan wrote to Sir Redvers Buller, Commander-in-Chief of Her Majesty's Forces in South Africa, offering five of his villas at Matjesfontein, to be used for accommodating about fifty wounded soldiers, as well as a donation of two hundred pounds a month for six months for the purpose of getting all the comforts that might be required for the wounded. He also mentioned that Dr Robertson of Matjesfontein was prepared to give his medical services free of charge. His offer was accepted, as was Dr. Robertson's.

The turret at Logan's hotel, which at that time housed a machine gun, became a lookout post. It was said of Logan that no soldier in uniform ever lacked a meal from his refreshment rooms - nor ever paid for one.

The Karoo cemetery at Pieter Meintjies on the Johannesburg-Cape Town National Road, usually referred to as 'The Monument', lies some twelve kilometres south of the village of Matjesfontein.

Among the graves in the cemetery, is that of Major-General Andrew Wauchope, the distinguished Commander of the Highland Brigade at the Battle of Magersfontein. Sadly, he was killed in action during this encounter, which proved to be so disastrous to the British War effort. It is from this distinctive memorial to the general that the nearby Monument Railway siding and Monument River, usually waterless in this arid, thirsty part of the Karoo, take their names.

Lord Methuen, under orders from the then British army commander, Sir Redvers Buller, was to move troops north up the railway line to relieve the siege at Kimberley. At Modder River, Methuen chose Wauchope and the Highland Brigade to spearhead an attack on the Magersfontein Kopje. It was believed that the Boer forces were camped on top of the kopje and British guns pounded the area. Wauchope is thought not to have been in favour of this plan of attack, but was overruled by Methuen. Shortly after midnight on December the 10th, 1899, Wauchope led the Highland Brigade, a body of four thousand men consisting of regiments of the Black Watch, the Seaforth Highlanders, the Argyll and Sutherland Highlanders and the Highland Light Infantry, into battle. They reportedly marched off into driving rain through mud, thorn bushes and clay.

However, the Boers had never been on top of the

Kopje, but were instead hidden at the foot of the hill in a nine-hundred-metre trench. Before the Highlanders were able to deploy, the Boers opened fire at almost point-blank range, decimating the Brigade. Trapped in the open for the whole day in the searing sun without food or water, the Highlanders became a sitting target.

Late in the day during an amnesty, among hundreds of dead and wounded soldiers, Wauchope's body was found by his aide-de-camp, Capt. Albert Rennie. He had been killed by a bullet over the left eye. Captain Rennie was not able to persuade the Boer ambulance to take Wauchope's body, so in desperation he secured the general's body to the outside of the ambulance with rope and followed it back to Modder River.

Wauchope was buried with full military honours at the British camp at Modder River at sunset on December the 12th, just two months after the outbreak of war. Pipers from each regiment of the Brigade preceded the body, on a stretcher borne by four Highlanders of the Black Watch.

On December the 17th the Hon. J. D. Logan, member of the Cape Legislature, arrived at Modder River.

Major John Buist relates:

'When J. D. Logan heard of the death of Wauchope he decided wisely, or unwisely, that it was inappropriate for this gallant, distinguished officer to be buried without due ceremony in so humble a resting place and obtained permission from Lord Methuen, who was then Chief of General Staff, to exhume the body and to have it re-interred at Matjesfontein. He also contacted Lady Wauchope in Scotland by telegraph, offering a vault at Matjesfontein for the burial of her husband. Lady Wauchope, possibly confused by the similarity of the names Magersfontein and Matjesfontein, is believed to have agreed to this at the time. Logan then travelled to Modder River by train himself; taking with him a handsome lead-lined coffin. He personally supervised the exhumation of Wauchope's body, which was placed in the coffin Logan had brought and put in Logan's compartment for the journey to Matjesfontein.'

On December the 19th, 1899, General Wauchope was buried at Matjesfontein, again with full military honours. The escort consisted of 11 officers and 195 non-commissioned officers, together with men of various detachments, including some of the Highland Brigade. A fife band complete with pipers had also been arranged.

A contemporary photograph shows the second burial to have been an event of pomp and circumstance. Standing out from the numerous mourners, were high-ranking British officers and representatives of the British government in South Africa. Many local inhabitants came to pay homage to a soldier who in death had become a national hero to many and who had won the respect even of his enemies. Among those present were Captain Rennie, A.D.C. to Wauchope, Colonel Schermbrucker, M.L.A., and Major Stuart, R.A., who was in charge of the funeral arrangements. The Logan family attended the funeral, together with others of note. The coffin was borne on a gun carriage, covered in wreaths, which was followed by the General's charger. The service was conducted by two army chaplains. On one of the wreaths was inscribed "A token of admiration and respect for one of Scotland's heroes, from his fellow countrymen at Matjesfontein". Logan paid for all the funeral expenses. The then head of the Wauchope family was Captain A.G. Wauchope, who later became Gen. Sir Arthur Grenfell Wauchope, G.C.B. G.C.M.G. CIE. D.S.O. High Commissioner and Commander-in-Chief, Palestine. He wrote:

'We are I think, all of one opinion that the moving of his body from Magersfontein was an error of judgement. At that time I was in hospital and not consulted...

In a letter Lady Wauchope, who was not able to be present at her husband's funeral, wrote:

'... the removal of my dear husband from Magersfontein to Matjesfontein was done without my knowledge - but I know it was done from the highest and best motives'. And finally she wrote 'Now that his remains are there, I feel I could not bear that they should be disturbed.'

Some years later in 1906, after the cessation of hostilities, she came to South Africa to visit his grave. Her impending visit aroused some apprehension in Cape Town among military and diplomatic circles, concerning Lady Wauchope's possible reactions to the interment of her distinguished husband in the remote environs of Matjesfontein. She was met in Cape Town by high-ranking military officers and civic dignitaries in a manner befitting the widow of one of England's most distinguished soldier heroes.

Their apprehensions proved to be groundless. At the graveside Lady Wauchope is said to have taken a long look at the Karoo stretching about her. She was moved to remark on its compelling loveliness, saying

'Indeed I am well satisfied that my Andrew rests here.

Logan was also instrumental in the release of George Wetton, the third member of the group of officers found guilty of atrocities against Boer prisoners in the infamous 'Breaker' Morant scandal and court martial. Wetton was not executed as were his colleagues Morant and Hancock, but was instead imprisoned in England. Logan was prominent in the campaign for Wetton's release from what many considered to have been a 'scapegoat' trial and the grossly unjust sentences handed down by the military tribunal. Logan met George Wetton in Cape Town while the latter was returning from prison to his native Australia.

In August 1901 in a debate in the British House of Commons, Mr. Joseph Chamberlain, the Prime Minister, justified Lord Roberts' declaration in December that the war was practically over ... for there had been nothing since but guerrilla warfare, and he hoped many of the troops would be home by September. For the Boers, continuation of the conflict had become increasingly difficult. Not only were they fighting for their very existence, but they were doing so at a time when supplies, obtained mainly from the Africans, had become extremely difficult to procure. Finding shelter had also become a major problem.

In early January 1902, unsubstantiated rumours of efforts to bring peace to a troubled South Africa abounded both in this country and overseas, but confirmation of this seemed to be lacking. Then, in this same month, an offer was made by the Dutch Government to mediate between the Boers and the British. This offer was turned down by the British.

Nevertheless Lord Kitchener sent a copy of the offer to the South African Republic leaders, who were granted permission to contact and confer with the former government of the Orange Free State. Twenty-two representatives of the two republics, under safe conduct, finally met at Vereeniging to formulate their conditions. These conditions were presented to Milner and Kitchener at Pretoria by the Boer delegates, Louis Botha, J.H. de la Rey, J.C. Smuts, Christiaan de Wet and Barry Hertzog. However, Milner and Kitchener had instructions to accept only unconditional surrender.

After a great deal of discussion the Boer delegates reported back to their colleagues at Vereeniging on the 29th of May. While some representatives were in favour of continuing the war, the majority wished for peace. Smuts stated his view that this course (of continuing the war) would be to 'sacrifice the Afrikaner nation itself upon the altar of independence'.

The decision to accept the British conditions was carried by fifty-four votes to six. Acting President of the South African Republic, Schalk Burger said:

'Here we stand at the graveside of the two Republics.'

A few minutes before midnight on May 31 1902, the Peace of Vereeniging was signed at Pretoria, allowing the country to stagger back to normality.

In terms of the peace treaty the two republics gave up their independence and recognised King Edward VII as their sovereign. Amnesty was granted for most of the rebels. No-one would receive the death sentence. All prisoners would be returned as swiftly as possible, subject to their signing the oath of allegiance to the British Crown. The Dutch language was guaranteed a degree of protection in the Law Courts. Britain promised three million pounds to repay the republics' war debts, and guaranteed property rights and relief aid.

A source of great regret to Milner was the fact that he was unable to extend the franchise to Africans before the new colonies were granted self-government. He was anxious to achieve a settlement as speedily as possible, and did not want to antagonise the Boers, nor indeed the English-speaking community, on this issue.

The war, which had been expected by Britain to last at most a few weeks, had dragged on for two and a half years at a monetary cost to Britain of two hundred million pounds; a cost in lives of about 22 000 British soldiers; and over 400 000 horses, mules and donkeys were expended!

The Boer losses were proportionately even more horrific. At least 7000 men died in action and an estimated 18 000 to 28 000 thousand lives, mostly those of women and children, were lost in concentration camps. The republics' farmlands were devastated, buildings destroyed, horses, cattle and sheep killed or looted.

As for the Africans, pawns in this struggle, few records were kept. Farm servants and their families, family retainers of well-to-do burghers, were also confined to concentration camps. They numbered 107000, and officially 7000 deaths were recorded, but a more realistic figure is probably 12 000. Then there were those Africans who fought for the British. They consisted of 10 000 armed scouts, guides and guards as well as 20 000 unarmed drivers and labourers. The

Boers admitted to shooting armed Africans, and in all probability unarmed Africans were also killed.

The outcome of the war could never have been in doubt. The Boer forces, vastly outnumbered in manpower and under-equipped in terms of armaments, had to succumb eventually to the rolling might of the British Empire.

During the war years Logan and Matjesfontein had proved their worth to the British Empire time after time. Among the many roles which Matjesfontein played during the war was a judicial role - General Scheepers, the captured Boer hero, was tried and convicted by the British in court proceedings held at Matjesfontein.

The Boers, who had lost the war, set themselves the task of winning the peace. Their cause, seemingly lost in 1902, steadily revived until the world saw Afrikaner nationalism triumph a half-century on.

Rhodes, circa 1894

CHAPTER XIV

A TOWERING PRESENCE

While the Anglo-Boer War was stumbling towards peace, the sands of life were running out for one of the towering figures of South African history, Cecil John Rhodes, Prime Minister of the Cape Colony from 1890 to 1895 and one of the most colourful, complex and enigmatic personalities ever to grace the African continent. Rhodes had never been able to recover politically or otherwise, from the ill-conceived and ill-fated Jameson Raid, which had effectively brought his Premiership to a premature and ignominious close.

To this day Rhodes' name is bedevilled by controversy, and his immense achievements are overshadowed by conflicting stories about his arrogance, his vanity and his ruthless pursuit of his own goals. The star by which Rhodes set his course was to extend the dominion of the British Empire over as much of Africa as possible. In the thinking of a century ago, when Africa seemed to be 'up for grabs' for all the nations of Europe, empire-building was seen by many to be a patriotic duty.

Cecil Rhodes' life has been well-documented in biographies and history books. He has been praised and vilified, loved and hated; in today's climate, when the task of the journalist and biographer seems to be as often as not, to expose the flaws in, if not actually denigrate, the characters of the great, his accomplishments have been largely overlooked.

Rhodes was born in the vicarage of Bishop

Stortford, in Lincolnshire, the third son of the local vicar, on the 5th of July 1853. At the age of seventeen, diagnosed as having weak lungs, he was advised by his doctor to take a long sea voyage.

To his delight he was sent by his parents to South Africa to join his older brother, Herbert, who was growing cotton in Natal. Accordingly, on September the first 1870, after a voyage of seventy-two days on a wooden ship, the Endora, he arrived at Durban. Two years later he proceeded to Kimberley to join Herbert at the diamond diggings. And it was on the mysterious African continent that young Rhodes was to make a fortune beyond the dreams of avarice, and to follow a calling and a destiny that would make his name famous throughout the civilized world.

As the mining of diamonds became more difficult and costly, many of the diggers were forced to amalgamate or to sell their claims. Rhodes and a friend, C. D. Rudd, went into partnership buying up claims, eventually forming the original De Beers Mining Company and building up over time an immensely profitable mining empire.

Rhodes was a relative latecomer to the goldfields of the Witwatersrand, haying believed at first that the gold there would not be found in any great quantities.

In 1887 he formed a company, the Goldfields of South Africa, later to become the Consolidated Goldfields of South Africa, one of South Africa's largest and most important mining houses.

As well as diamonds and gold, his sights were set upon opening up to Britain the vast tracts of land to the north. To this end he formed a company, the British South Africa Company, and managed in 1889 to obtain a charter from the British Government giving him the authority, at his own expense, to obtain land and mineral rights in the territories later to become Southern and Northern Rhodesia.

Rhodes became Prime Minister of the Cape Colony almost by accident. In 1890 Prime Minister John Sprigg was defeated in Parliament. The only organised party in Parliament was the Afrikaner Bond, led by J.H. Hofmeyr, holding approximately forty percent of the seats. The remainder were held by small groups with conflicting policies. As Hofmeyr refused to form a ministry himself the Governor Sir Henry Loch sent for Rhodes who, successful, wealthy, powerful and with the gift of drawing both Dutch and English to his ventures, seemed the appropriate man to lead the government.

Cecil John Rhodes had realised that, in order to fulfil his dreams to ' settle the earth with Anglo Saxons' and to unite the Cape Colony and Natal with the Transvaal and the Orange Free State in South Africa, he must have some voice in Government.

This meant entering the Cape Colony Parliament and he achieved this by capturing the seat at Barkly West, having failed to obtain the nomination for a Kimberley seat. He remained the member for Barkly West for the rest of his life.

Rhodes had had no ambitions for the Premiership, but a friendly administration at the Cape was of prime importance to his plans and he immediately accepted the position when it was offered him. The Bond promised to give him a fair chance at governing the colony and he gathered together his first ministry, which comprised a number of talented and capable men: John X. Merriman, an old friend from the early Kimberley days, was made Treasurer; J.W. Sauer became Colonial Secretary; James Sivewright, a personal friend and a successful speculator, who was also an expert on electricity, became the new Commissioner for Public Works; P.H. Faure, a shrewd Dutch lawyer, was given the portfolio of Native Affairs; Sir James Rose-Innes a much-respected lawyer, was made Attorney-General. Rhodes' cabinet thus consisted of three former Opposition members and two from the Bond. His slogan was 'the government of South Africa by the people of South Africa with the Imperial flag for defence'. Rhodes hoped for eventual union with the republics and thought that this could principally be achieved by means of the Railway, the Customs Union and a common Native policy, as well as through various educational institutions.

In 1891 Rhodes first rented a large old house in Cape Town called "Groote Schuur" (meaning "Big Barn"), which dated back to the days of the old Dutch East India Company. He bought the property some two years later and decided to renovate and live in it.

The task of restoring the house he entrusted to a young British architect, Herbert Baker. Baker was particularly interested in Dutch Colonial architecture and in Groote Schuur, he produced a masterpiece. Baker was also sent round the country to find and buy old furniture with which to refurbish Groote Schuur. It was Rhodes who gave Herbert Baker his great chance, and Baker has left behind a wealth of magnificent architecture in South Africa.

Rhodes further bought up surrounding farms as

they became available and established gardens, where the public was allowed to wander and picnic, provided they left no litter. The mountain was his refuge, a chapel and a retreat where he would think and meditate. Though not a churchgoer Rhodes was deeply religious. He once confided in Baker that he was really 'saying his prayers' when he was out riding or just sitting on Table Mountain.

A young Englishman, H. E. V. Pickstone, recounts his introduction to Rhodes and his partner, Rudd. Pickstone had spent some time in California working on fruit farms and he felt that South African conditions would be favourable for fruit farming. Through Rudd he met Rhodes, who, on learning of his knowledge of and skill in fruit farming, immediately instructed him to buy 'the whole Drakenstein Valley'. However, Pickstone was content to buy several farms to start with, and not the whole valley! He was later to become the first manager of the Rhodes Fruit Farm Company.

Rhodes built a model village for the coloured labourers and Hottentots on the estate, with a church, a school and a house for the pastor. He also introduced Arab stallions to improve the horse-breeding industry.

In 1895, after five years of successful administration, despite the catering contract debacle and the consequent resignation of key government ministers, Rhodes seemed to have maintained his grip on power However, a further crisis now loomed - the grievances of the "Uitlanders" in the Transvaal had by now reached such a pitch, that drastic remedies were called for, causing many schemes to be mooted by way of a solution. The scheme which was finally settled upon and which led to the Jameson Raid, was to have serious international repercussions and devastate Rhodes' political career.

The planning of the Raid, of which Joseph Chamberlain, the new Colonial Secretary, was certainly aware, has been minutely recorded and dissected in countless publications. It is sufficient to record here, that after the Raid Rhodes immediately resigned his premiership and proceeded to England, arriving on February the 4th 1896, to be called to account for his part in the Raid.

Should he have been found guilty of complicity in the Raid, it seemed as if Joseph Chamberlain would also have been forced to accept some responsibility for what had happened, unless Rhodes could exonerate him. Chamberlain, whose position within the British government would have been seriously compromised in this event, found it expedient to state the following in defence of Rhodes and the Charter Company, in a debate in the House of Commons on February the 13th of that year:

'I say to the best of my knowledge that Mr. Rhodes, that the Chartered Company, that the Reform Committee of Johannesburg, and the High Commissioner were all equally ignorant of the intention or action of Dr. Jameson.'

His meaning was plain - his contention was that nobody actually knew what Jameson would do until he did it.

However, an enquiry was demanded not only by the House of Commons but also by the Cape Assembly. Before the enquiry could take place, the Matabele uprising against the Charter Company, starting with the slaughter of all whites within reach, caused Rhodes to depart immediately for Rhodesia, where he was involved in organising relief for those areas under threat and for initiating counter attacks against the Matabele. From April to October 1886, despite suffering another severe bout of malaria, he devoted himself selflessly to finding a solution to the conflict and bringing peace to the region, displaying great courage, wisdom and patience in the process.

Repression was obviously not the answer and Rhodes had to find an alternative to bring peace and settle the grievances of the Matabele. He set about negotiating, in what turned out to be a long drawn out process, a settlement that was fair and agreeable to all; and peace was finally established in October 1896.

It was around this time that Lewis Michell, his devoted friend and financial advisor visited him in Bulawayo; and one day drove in a Cape cart to Rhodes' new estate in the Matopos. From there one morning Rhodes and Michell climbed a bare, slippery granite hill to see the exact spot where Rhodes desired to be buried. It is a strange coincidence that another great South African personality, Olive Schreiner, also selected her own lonely burial site on a rocky hill.

Rhodes seemed convinced that he could save the Charter by protecting Chamberlain and shielding Chamberlain's reputation; he steadfastly denied that Chamberlain had played any part in the planning of the Raid. He was therefore prepared to accept full responsibility. He would attend the enquiry himself; but would not permit any of the evidence germane to the matter which he possessed, in the way of telegrams and messages between himself and Chamberlain, to be used. He left Cape Town in January 1897 accompanied by his sister, Edith; by coincidence Olive Schreiner was travelling to England on the same ship with her novel, “Trooper Peter Halket of Mashonaland”.

Whilst awaiting the enquiry in London, Rhodes saw Jameson again, for the first time since the Raid, and their friendship was resumed. For the rest of his life Rhodes regarded Jameson, who became a constant companion, as the only doctor in whose advice he could really trust.

It was ill health which drove Rhodes to South Africa. Perhaps it was ill health which caused his error in judgment in promoting the Raid, the sense of time passing too rapidly. His heart was not sound and successive bouts of malaria had progressively weakened him. As early as 1896 he had been told that his life would be short.

The enquiry found no justification for Rhodes’ behaviour, although it admitted genuine grievances on the behalf of the “Uitlanders”. An absolute and unqualified condemnation was expressed of the Raid. Rhodes was urged by his friends to release the cables which would exonerate him at the expense of Chamberlain. This he refused to do.

In a subsequent debate in the House of Commons, in July, Chamberlain declared ‘The Government do not intend to abolish the Charter’, a statement with which Rhodes was satisfied.

On returning to South Africa Rhodes contrived to keep out of politics. However, he was concerned at the time that the victims of the Raid should be fully compensated by him and was as a result inundated with claims. Despite his efforts to retrieve the situation, the rift between the Dutch and English settlers, widened still further as a result of the Jameson Raid.

Rhodes' break with the Afrikaner Bond was final and in addition, by now many English-speaking South Africans had turned against him.

He was reinstated on the board of the Charter Company, but the company had of late been greatly restricted and left with much reduced powers. Rhodes was unable to attend the opening of the Bulawayo Mafeking Railway, a project he had initiated, owing to malaria and heart trouble. He was preoccupied with extending the railway and telegraph systems east and west and north and south across Africa. He reached an agreement with the German Government for a telegraph route through German East Africa, Tanganyika, in March 1899. He met the Kaiser and liked him to the extent that he included German scholars in his scholarship scheme in his will.

Indeed his will was a great preoccupation with Rhodes during the last few years of his life. A fervent believer in education, he had established the School of Mines in Kimberley, and hoped to be able to help establish a university at Cape Town.

Rhodes himself was not only a man of high intelligence, but also an intellectual and even in a sense a frustrated scholar, pursuing an academic career throughout his life where circumstance permitted. In fact a few years after his arrival in South Africa, he had managed to pay his way to Oxford and enroll at Oriel College for a term.

However, his academic career was broken by the necessity of his having to earn a living, and he completed the next term only in 1876, eventually finishing his last term in 1881. Oxford captivated him. He read avidly, debated and made some lifelong friends. The dream of Oxford remained with him his entire life. So imbued was he with the spirit of the university, that years later in his will he created a Trust to enable students from all over the British Empire and America to obtain scholarships for Oxford. These were awarded to sixty scholars from the Colonies, and two from each of the states of the United States. He was concerned that there should be no unfair discrimination in the granting of these scholarships and stated categorically that 'no student shall be qualified or disqualified for election to a scholarship on account of his race or religious opinions.' In a letter he wrote 'the last thing I want is a bookworm.' The requisites were to be literary and scholastic achievement, as well as manly sports, qualities of manhood and moral force of character.

As well as many other bequests to families, friends, employees and institutions, he left Groote Schuur and one thousand pounds a year for its maintenance to the Federal Prime Minister of South Africa when Union should be achieved.

He was to be buried in the Matopos and a monument in memory of those who died in the First Matabele War was also to be erected there.

After a period of relative political inactivity following the Jameson Raid, Rhodes decided to contest the General Election of 1898, however, and retained his Barkly West seat. He was also nominated and elected as member for Namaqualand. In the prelude to the Anglo-Boer War of 1899, he was convinced that Kruger would climb down and that war would be averted, a political mistake as serious and grievous as his tacit support of the Jameson Raid in 1895 and a mistake which was to haunt him for the rest of his life.

Regarded with deep suspicion by former friends, Rhodes kept aloof from any war mongering, and in Parliament addressed other issues including the 'native problem'. In terms of 'the native problem', he simply reiterated his policy of 'equal rights for every civilised man south of the Zambezi', thereby rather ironically defending the natives' right to vote against Prime Minister Schreiner's attempts to disenfranchise them.

By September of 1899, war seemed inevitable. Even before the declaration Rhodes had intended to leave for Kimberley, and he arrived there the day after the outbreak of hostilities. Two days later Kimberley was under siege. Rhodes not only took charge of all De Beers affairs in Kimberley, but, using employees from De Beers, succeeded in erecting a fort on the outskirts of Kimberley and in forming a cavalry unit. He checked supplies, established a soup kitchen, supplied milk and fruit to the troops and military hospital, and kept ten thousand Africans employed on road-making and other public works. He was even inclined to disregard the commander Col. Kekewich on occasion and to make and carry out his own decisions in matters military. Rhodes is reputed to have been responsible for many defence measures which helped to save Kimberley, demonstrating an immense practical genius. When the town was threatened by the Boer artillery, he had one of his mining engineers construct a gun, known as "Long Cecil", with which to retaliate!

The town was relieved on February the 15th 1900

by a force commanded by General French. Rhodes' great efforts during the siege did not go unnoticed or unrewarded. A campaign medal awarded to Rhodes posthumously was received by his brother, Frank, on behalf of "Colonel the Right Honourable Cecil Rhodes" and a letter conveying His Majesty's 'high appreciation of the services rendered by the late officer during the recent campaign'.

After the siege Rhodes spent many months in his beloved Rhodesia, keeping in touch with the war from a distance, and occasionally offering advice to Milner, in whom he had great confidence; and as well formulating his plans for the north and for South Africa after the war. At this stage the British forces expected the war to be over very soon. Rhodes spent many hours walking, riding, shooting game, visiting the settlers and simply chatting and gossiping, whilst in Rhodesia. He spent Christmas and New Year in Cape Town and travelled to London in July 1901 on De Beers and Chartered Company business.

There he saw a heart specialist who confirmed that his condition was serious, and advised 'rest and travel'. Accordingly, with his great friends Jameson, Beit, Metcalfe and Jourdan, Rhodes set out for the continent, though his heart condition continued to trouble him.

For many months Rhodes had been plagued by the unwelcome attentions of an adventuress, Princess Catherine Maria Radziwill, who had succeeded in ingratiating herself with many people in high places. There are numerous accounts to be found of this extraordinary woman, her intrigues, her mischief making, her alleged forgeries of Rhodes' signature and letters; leading to her eventual downfall.

In January 1902 Rhodes decided that, ill as he was, he must return to Cape Town from Europe, as he was required to give evidence in the forgery case against Princess Radziwill. Rhodes was a dying man by now, though few realised this. Alfred Lord Milner still saw Rhodes, rather ironically, as the next Prime Minister of the Cape Colony.

At the end of February Rhodes gave evidence repudiating Princess Radziwill's alleged forgeries, driving to Cape Town from his seaside cottage at Muizenberg. By now his intimate friends knew how desperately ill he was, and only close friends were allowed to see him. A last wish to travel once more to England, was to remain unfulfilled. The ship on which a cabin had been prepared for Rhodes, sailed from Cape Town on the day of his death, which took place in Muizenberg on March the 26th 1902.

Two of Rhodes' closest friends, Jameson and Lewis Michell, were with him until the end. Michell, sitting with Rhodes while Jameson took a brief rest, heard him murmur the famous words 'so little done, so much to do.'

Rhodes was accorded a state funeral in Cape Town, the Archbishop basing his address on the text "Know ye not that that there is a prince and a great man fallen this day in Israel?" The coffin, loaded with flowers, was then put on Rhodes' own train and conveyed by stages to Bulawayo; at each halt there were mourners and flowers. One of the stops was at Matjesfontein where Emma and Gertrude Logan laid a wreath. After a second funeral at Bulawayo the coffin was transported to the Matopos where a grave had been dug: and the burial took place. Thousands of Matabele lined the way, and accorded Rhodes the royal salute “Bayete”, which had never before been given any white man.

Milner wrote, when he heard of Rhodes’ imminent death, that ‘certainly there has never been a time since first I came to South Africa when I have wanted him more.’

CHAPTER XV

KING WILLOW AGAIN

Discussions had taken place regarding the possibility of sending another South African cricket team to England in the summer of 1900; and Logan had offered to finance the tour. At the Annual Meeting of the Transvaal Cricket Union, held at the Wanderers Club on August the 23rd 1899, this offer was welcomed and a vote of thanks proposed to Logan for his 'sportsmanlike conduct in offering to finance the South African team in England'.

The profits of Lord Hawke's fourth cricket tour to South Africa earlier in the year amounted to about seventy pounds. This was announced at the Annual General Meeting of the South African Cricket Association on September the 30th, also held at the Wanderers. It was announced at the same time that this sum would accrue to the Association.

That great promoter of cricket, Lord Hawke, had offered to arrange the fixtures for the South African team. Lord Hawke announced in December of the same year that the Yorkshire County committee planned to make provisions for its professional cricketers in their old age. Attention had to be drawn to their plight, described thus:

'Many cases had come to light of men who were idols of the cricket public in their day ... who having lost their skills for one reason or another ... had drifted into destitution ...'

Yorkshire had also introduced a scheme of remuneration for professional cricketers in the winter months.

May 1899 was to be the last occasion upon which Matjesfontein was to celebrate Queen Victoria's birthday. As usual, the day was declared a holiday, beginning with a cricket match, then a twenty-one gun salute, a luncheon and sports; followed by fireworks in the evening. After a reign of sixty-three years the queen was to die in January 1901, to be greatly mourned throughout the British Empire.

With the advent of war there were doubts as to whether South Africa would be able to field a team; the cricketers being scheduled to leave in March 1900.

In the event, this cricket team, which was referred to in the press as 'the South Africans', 'the Colonials' and 'Logan's team', toured England and Scotland in the 1901 season. The team was captained by Murray Bisset and among the fifteen players comprising the team was young Jimmy Logan junior, who played in twelve innings' and averaged fifteen runs.

Logan had rented Dalguise Castle in Scotland and here he entertained the South African team. During the shooting season Colonel Schermbrucker, now close on eighty years old, also stayed with Logan.

A contemporary account testifies to the athletic capabilities of this remarkable man, saying that he at such an advanced age, 'foots it over the heather with almost as light a foot as does his sure-shooting host who has hardly reached half his years.'

The tour lasted for three months and the South Africans played almost thirty matches. Murray Bisset, when interviewed at Cardiff, described the tour as having successfully popularised cricket in South Africa; the side had improved immensely owing to the experience gained. They had been received with marked cordiality. Out of twenty-five matches the South Africans had won thirteen, lost nine and drawn three. The match against the Marylebone Cricket Club was probably the most important of the tour. And Logan's team, though losing, gave a good account of themselves. The special reporter accompanying the team wrote, 'Two of the greatest ambitions of the sports-loving youth of South Africa ... those who love cricket and the Sport of Kings ... have been to play at Lords and to see the Derby. Well, eleven of us have realised both of these ambitions and are prepared to die happy!'

The tour was certainly not all work and no play.

There were race meetings, theatres, Henley boat races and many other diversions. The first win by the South Africans was against the London County Cricket Club, fielding greats such as W.G. Grace and W.R. Murdoch. The L.C.C.C. made the South Africans honorary members, and entertained them to an after match dinner at the Crystal Palace, which was sadly later to be razed by fire.

J.D. Logan spoke at the dinner, as did Colonel Schermbrucker and Murray Bissett, the team captain, to such good effect that a writer in one of the London dailies wrote, 'If the Africans can bat, bowl and field as well as they can talk, their success is assured!'

The Surrey County Cricket Club gave a banquet for the South Africans, at which Logan replied to the toast 'The South African team' and Murray Bissett proposed a toast to the hosts.

A traveller writing to the *Cape Times* in July, complained bitterly about the food on Cape Railways, asserting:

'... meals are irregularly procured at the various stations, happy the man who takes a hamper. The Contractor who feeds the travelling public in the Cape Colony is away playing cricket in England. Better for him that he stayed behind and supervised the meat and vegetable supply of his score of refreshment rooms. When his term of office is up he will have many enemies and possibly some competition. He deserves them ... The worst fed passengers on earth are to be found in the trains of the C.G.R. The war is no excuse ...'

Before leaving for the Cape in October, Jimmy, Emma and Gertrude Logan attended a recital of sacred music in Houndwood Church, at which Logan presented a new organ to the congregation.

In making the presentation Logan said he remembered as a boy being made to walk two or three miles each way to Houndwood Church every Sunday, to attend the services of the late minister there. He told the gathering further that this was the first time he had ever spoken in Church, though his voice had been heard often enough in Parliament. It gave him great pleasure, though not being a musical man himself, to afford the people of his old church the means of enjoying good music!

About this time Logan also purchased a house for his brother in Reston to be called "Karoo House", an unexpected appellation to find in the main street of a small Scottish border town. In 1991 this house, which for several years had in part been converted into a general store, was put up for sale.

The advertisement reads:

'Occupying a prominent position, this large Victorian residence, Karoo House, must be considered a rarity on the market. The house enjoys a wealth of character with its attractive marble fireplace and spacious reception rooms, four bedrooms, kitchen, study, box room, bathroom, garage, gardens. Offers invited in the region of £65.000.'

Emma and Gertrude Logan dressed in the style of the day

The Coffee Shop

Photograph of Barrydale in the Karoo, not far from Matiiesfontein

CHAPTER XVI

THE BELMONT HOTEL

Ceres was yet another South African village to have earned a reputation as a health resort. Laid out in 1854, it had long attracted tourists, invalids, prospectors and sportsmen. When Logan purchased the property, Belmont, a chateau of hewn stone set in seventy-five acres of woodland, he saw its potential as a hotel and sanatorium. The gardens were well laid out and included a lake, a croquet lawn and a 'double' tennis court. Inside, Logan installed acetylene gas lighting, as well as the latest in laundry and plumbing. A well-known firm of interior decorators, D. Isaacs and Co. of Cape Town, were hired to refurbish and furnish the rooms. There was a billiard room and a smoking room; and the ladies' drawing room was described in the *Worcester Standard* as 'a dream of loveliness'.

The crowning accolade to Jimmy Logan's career must have been the invitations that he and Emma Logan received to the coronation of King Edward VII and Queen Alexandra on June the 26th, 1902. The magnificent court dress that Logan wore and Emma's beautiful gown are still to be seen in the museum at Matjiesfontein. This event, to which all the crowned heads of Europe were invited, was the scene of pageantry that has passed forever from the world stage. Never again would so many royal houses be represented.

In 1903 Jimmy Logan was elected as representative of the Western Cape Division in the Legislative Assembly. In that election L.S. Jameson, who succeeded Sir John Sprigg as Prime Minister, had a small majority of five in the Lower House and a majority of only one in the Higher House, an awkward situation to be in in any parliament. In this way it came about that J.D. Logan held the balance of power in the Higher House. Though elected as a Progressive he had always shown himself to be an independent thinker. Logan did not agree with the Progressive standpoint with regard to the tax on diamonds, as he considered this would be detrimental to the country as a whole. He also disagreed with the bill for additional representation of constituencies in the Lower House. And in May 1904, in spite of their entreaties, Logan left the Progressive Party in the lurch by visiting England once more. Lord de Villiers, the Chief Justice, had to be called upon for a deciding vote in the Higher House on not only this but other bills in order to save the ministry, whose policy he incidentally did not support, from breaking up completely.

In politics Logan expressed his standpoint so forcefully at times that he antagonised many political friends and made many political enemies. It was in September 1907 that matters finally came to a head.

The parties, Progressive and Afrikaner Bond, were so evenly balanced in the Upper House that when the Council went into Committee and a Progressive took the Chair, Logan held the balance of power.

On this date the council went into Committee on the Estimates, and Logan consistently blocked progress, voting with the opposition until on

September 17th, Dr. Jameson announced that the Government would ask the Governor to suspend both Houses of Parliament, in order to solve the constitutional deadlock in the Legislative Council. A general Council election followed and the Jameson Ministry was defeated after four years in power. Jameson was to be succeeded by John X. Merriman as Prime Minister.

Two years before Union Logan withdrew from politics to devote his energies to his catering enterprises and to Matjiesfontein.

J.D. Logan junior (Jim Logan)

CHAPTER XVII

FAMILY MATTERS

Gertrude's brother, Jimmy, had taken over the management of the Milner Hotel without any great success. In 1908 he married a certain Mrs. Bramley, a widow with two children. This marriage seemed to cause a rift between father and son. Perhaps J.D. Logan had wished for a younger bride for his son unencumbered with the children of a former marriage. Whatever the reasons behind the rift, it was too great to be bridged. A former schoolmate of Jimmy junior's, Tom Leask, invited the newlyweds to stay with him on his parents' farm at Krugersdorp. The Leasks subsequently offered Jimmy junior employment on their farm and the young couple decided to move to Klerksdorp, where they eventually bought a farm of their own. This domestic upheaval may well have contributed to J.D. Logan's withdrawal from politics in the same year.

On a voyage back from England in 1905 Gertrude Logan met and became engaged to, Major Herbert John Buist of the Royal Army Medical Corps. This was to be a long engagement – the marriage did not take place until 1912.

In marked contrast to Jimmy junior's marriage, the union between Gertrude and Herbert Buist in 1912 was to be celebrated in grand style, taking place as it did at Matjesfontein itself with all the ceremony and happiness that might be desired.

Herbert Buist was in charge of all the military medical services in South Africa. He and Gertrude lived at Roberts Heights, now Voortrekkerhoogte, until the outbreak of war in 1914, when he was transferred to Cape Town and given an office in The Castle.

The couple were living in Kenilworth when their son John was born in October 1914.

However, Buist was transferred back to England in 1915, and Gertrude and their baby accompanied him. Herbert Buist was then posted to Salonika and attached to the French Army. After the war he became Deputy Director of Medical Services in the Scottish Army.

After they had settled in Scotland J.D. Logan did visit the Buists and was further acquainted with his small grandson. But he was not a well man, suffering by now from acute dropsy. Gertrude Logan sailed to South Africa in 1920 to spend some time with her father in his last days and was at his bedside when he died in July 1920.

He was buried in the little cemetery at Pieter Meintjies near Matjesfontein in the limitless Karoo which had cast its spell over him so many years before. He would not have asked for more.

Herbert Buist, now Colonel Buist, retired from the army in 1921; whereupon he and Gertrude and their son returned to South Africa, to Matjesfontein, where they made Tweedside their home. 'Little did I think I would settle here in 1921 after thirty years as an army surgeon,' Colonel Buist once remarked, 'Yet it grows on you and you get to like it. I don't know why the time passes so fast, or what I have been doing, but I never have an idle day!'

The Karoo after a painting by Tony Grogan

Matjiesfontein Station

CHAPTER XVIII

A CLUTCH OF GHOSTS

It is perhaps inevitable that Matjiesfontein, steeped as it is in history, and visited down the years by a variety of exceptional personalities, should be haunted by its own past. For haunted it is said to be. A goodly number of people, both local and foreign, have stories to tell of these Matjiesfontein spirits.

Reassuringly for Matjiesfontein, most recorded encounters with these denizens of the Shadow World seem to have been with somewhat jovial spirits.

A former member of the staff, who happened to be working alone in the Lord Milner Hotel before the present refurbished Lord Milner had opened, was awakened one night by a noise at the hotel door. There was a small group of people, curiously dressed she thought, for travellers seeking accommodation. They seemed as surprised to see her as she was to see them, for there had been no sound of approaching traffic and they were strangers. She stared at them. They stared blankly back, then looked in a puzzled manner at one another. Then she noticed that the lower parts of their bodies seemed to be disappearing. Minutes later they had vanished to the sound of distant and fading laughter. The rest was silence.

Then, much more recently, Jennifer Buist, J. D. Logan's great-granddaughter, was in one of Tweedside Lodge's many rooms, when she heard a movement at the door. At first, assuming it to be a Karoo zephyr, she ignored it. But not when the door started rattling. She went to the door and opened it. The air was still; there was no breeze. What then had caused the rattle? Suddenly the balmy air became chill. Cold air came into the room and moved past her towards the open window, which now began to shake violently as the invisible force passed through it into the outside world. This was a ghost who certainly knew his or her way about. Perhaps the whole episode was a case of experiencing a ghost that was sensed rather than seen.

There are said to be other ghosts at the Lodge. The Logan family have come to know these mostly nocturnal visitors well. Sounds are heard in the night. There are bumps in distant rooms; there is faint laughter and the tinkle of convivial glasses; and again the rattle at the doors. This sound invariably ceases when the door is opened by a member of the family and the ghost is permitted to enter; or perhaps move out into a wider world.

There is another more poignant voice out of Matjiesfontein's past. That other soldier. A thought with which to conjure. Legend or reality? That famous young, mysterious, other soldier with the blood-soaked bandage about his head? The very stuff of Africa, be he legend, or as others have insisted, merely a reality sprung from the strange soil of the Karoo.

Yes, there were those who were indeed aware of 'the other mysterious soldier'. Down the years many have claimed to see him. Motorists have told of glimpses of him from car headlights. A few travellers have reported daylight sightings.

Through the years the description hardly varies; stained, khaki tunic, leggings, bandaged head, pallid sunken cheeks. Above all there is a general consensus of a sad loneliness, a yearning to communicate, to cross the barrier from beyond the grave. And then, swiftly, silently, the soldier was gone, not to be seen again perhaps for years.

A more recent reported sighting of the mysterious soldier might be interpreted as something of an international confirmation of sorts. This occurred when two young women in the office of the British military attaché in Pretoria were travelling by car to Cape Town. As they neared Matjiesfontein the driver saw what she took to be a uniformed soldier sitting at the roadside. She was horrified to observe a bloodstained bandage about his head, and that his arm was in a sling. But the other girl could see nothing. They stopped and hurried to offer help. But as they neared the soldier, he vanished. When they later related the sighting, their hosts were able to confirm that the phantom soldier had indeed been seen on a number of occasions. And the description was always the same to the last detail, even down to the sad searching eyes.

On their return journey, passing the cemetery, the girl who previously had not seen him called out 'Why, there's your soldier!' But this time the driver could not see the soldier.

Then, some years ago when John Buist was dining at a famous Cape Town club he heard a woman seated at the next table mention the soldier and the cemetery. John was unable to resist introducing himself and explaining that the cemetery was on his farm. The woman had a strange story to tell him.

One day she had to drive alone to Beaufort West. Her husband warned her sternly that, as she was alone, she was not to offer lifts to any hitchhikers. As she approached the famous cemetery she saw a soldier standing near the road. His head was bandaged, his arm was in a sling. She was tempted to offer him a lift. As she drove slowly by, she observed the sadness in his eyes.

She decided she must offer him a ride and reversed, but before she reached the spot, she saw in her mirror that he had disappeared. She did not see him again.

Joan du Plooy, for many years a staff member at the Lord Milner Hotel, has written about the soldier, 'Several travellers have told of sighting a soldier leaning over the cemetery gate as they have passed by, usually at dusk.' She then raises a query others have suggested. 'Could it be General Wauchope himself seeking to return to Magersfontein to join his men who fell in the battle?'

Old soldier, young soldier? One soldier or two? Who knows?

The soldier has not been seen for some years now but some of those local people who knew of him are convinced that he will come again.

For the sceptics perhaps Shakespeare's famous lines, as spoken by Hamlet to Horatio, would apply. Hamlet has been relating some ghostly experiences and says to the sceptical Horatio: 'There are more things in heaven and earth, Horatio, than are dreamt of in your philosophy.'

A delightful ghost story appeared in a recent issue of the central Karoo newsletter, *Rose's Roundup.*

A touring group of Scots pipers gathered at Matjiesfontein recently to pay tribute to the memory of Major-General Andrew "Red Mick" Wauchope, who is buried about ten kilometres south of the village.

The lads played a stimng tribute to the general at the cemetery, sipped a few drams of the good stuff and played a few more tributes. After several sessions of piping and refreshments, one of the Scots lay down in the shade of a nearby tree to rest, and fell asleep.

When he woke some hours later darkness had fallen and his companions had left. Undeterred, he decided to walk to the Lord Milner Hotel. So he picked up his pipes and strolled back, playing a few Scottish laments as he went, just to pass the time.

Not far away on the busy national highway, a family had stopped for a break in their journey and a picnic supper. As they spread their rug and opened their picnic basket, they were horrified to see a wild Scot emerge from the little graveyard wearing full regalia and filling the night air with the wail of his pipes.

Our bonnie Scot was equally mystified to see a whole family suddenly bundling their possessions into their car and speeding off into the night in a state of obvious panic.

Later, when a local farmer offered him a lift to the hotel and heard the story, the farmer burst out laughing. He explained that the area was rich with the stones of ghosts from the old South African War days.

The terrified family must have had quite a tale to tell when they got home!

It's a great boost for the legend of Red Mick.

General Wauchope's tomb and J.D. Logan's grave (foreground)

General Wauchope's headstone

David Rawdon buys Matjiesfontein - a contemporary comment

CHAPTER XIX

HIBERNATION

Even before James Douglas Logan died in 1920, the exuberant tempo of Matjesfontein was fading. With the end of World War I had come quieter, almost anticlimactic times. After his father's death, J. D. Logan junior, who had been farming in the Klerksdorp area, came to administer the family's extensive interests from Reston Villa at Matjesfontein. He had earned a reputation as a botanist and it was he who established the Karoo Aloe Garden at Whitehills station, north of Matjesfontein.

An interested participant in the Aloe Garden venture was the then General Manager of Railways, Sir William Hoy, himself a keen conservationist. A story told by the late Professor Brian Rycroft, former director of Kirstenbosch Botanic Gardens, recalls that Sir William instructed the station master at Matjesfontein, 'Once a week you will catch the northbound train at Matjesfontein and get off at Whitehills station.' 'And what do I do there, Sir William?' 'You water the aloes'. 'And after I've watered the aloes, Sir William?' 'Why you wait for the southbound of course, and you get off at Matjesfontein. And you do this once weekly'. And this is exactly what happened.

However, once the National Road came into being, Whitehills was too far off the beaten track to attract visitors and the Karoo Aloe Garden was moved to Worcester Some of the plants originally from the aloe garden at Tweedside Lodge, may still be seen at the now-silent little station at Whitehills. Two succulents that Jimmy Logan discovered are named after him.

Jimmy junior also owned one of the largest collections of big game heads in South Africa, a male and female head of every possible species.

A life member of the Western Province Cricket Club, Jim Logan was a well-known cricketer in his younger days. He was a member of that South African team, sponsored by his father, which toured England in 1901 under the Captaincy of Murray Bisset. This team made 692 against Cambridge University. On this tour Jim Logan reputedly stood up to the bowling of W.G. Grace!

From 1920 until his death in January 1960, aged 79, Jim Logan lived at Reston Villa. Some years before his death, he decided that a great deal of his father's personal papers should be destroyed, and sadly as a result much of historical value and interest was reduced to ashes. The hotel has been leased to various people and organisations down the years, including the South African Breweries from 1920 to 1930. But the magic of the Logan years was gone; the only glories now were memories.

The downfall of one manager was caused by his excessive 'generosity'. He gave away most of the hotel's stock of whisky to passing travellers. Another manager, a German, had a son who had been in the German Cavalry in World War I. On occasion this young man would drink not wisely but too well, then don his German Cavalry uniform, and, with drawn sword, chase the local populace! He had to be arrested and put in the police cell to sober up.

The little village and hotel entered a period of hibernation that lasted for nearly half a century. As much as the railways had contributed immensely to the birth of Matjesfontein, so did roads and road transport almost cause its demise.

The invention of the motor car and the improvement of roads increased the range of transport, and made more destinations available to travellers. A stop at Matjesfontein on the long journey northwards became unnecessary. Motorists impatient to reach their destinations scarcely gave the village a second glance. When, shortly after World War II, the new main road was built bypassing the village, Matjesfontein sank into the obscurity common to so many other shabby country hotels.

Mr. Piet Olivier, manager of the Milner Hotel before David Rawdon bought the village, described the population thus: 'Well, let's see, there's my wife, myself, the Buists, Willie Marais (who himself pumped petrol for visiting motorists), a few railway families... oh, about fifty. But things are very quiet here. You see these cards on the counter (in the bar) ... my wife and I play most of the day. The loser has to shuffle'.

Sometimes the only movement seems to be the heat waves caressing the buildings. Matjiesfontein has been described as the only town where doves cross the street, looking neither to right nor left.

'The village was neglected and the hotel degraded to a dusty overnight joint for travelling reps used to indifferent accommodation and even more indifferent food' reported Ann Starke in the *Fair Lady* of February the 19th, 1970.

Railway gangers and pensioners lived in the old cottages at a rental of four rands a month.

The hotel was reduced to a profit of seventeen rands a month. Its main supporters, it is said, were two drunks, a government official and a local farmer. Then the official was transferred, the farmer shot himself and the economy of the hotel was in the red!

On the death of his uncle, Jimmy Logan, who was also laid to rest in the cemetery at Pieter Meintjies, Major John Buist, recently retired from the British Army, inherited the estate.

Major Buist subsequently decided to sell the village because in its unsatisfactory state, 'it was a great responsibility to try to keep it from dwindling away into complete disrepair.' To "keep up its face" money had to be spent on the village, but there were few people who could afford to pay the rentals that would result.

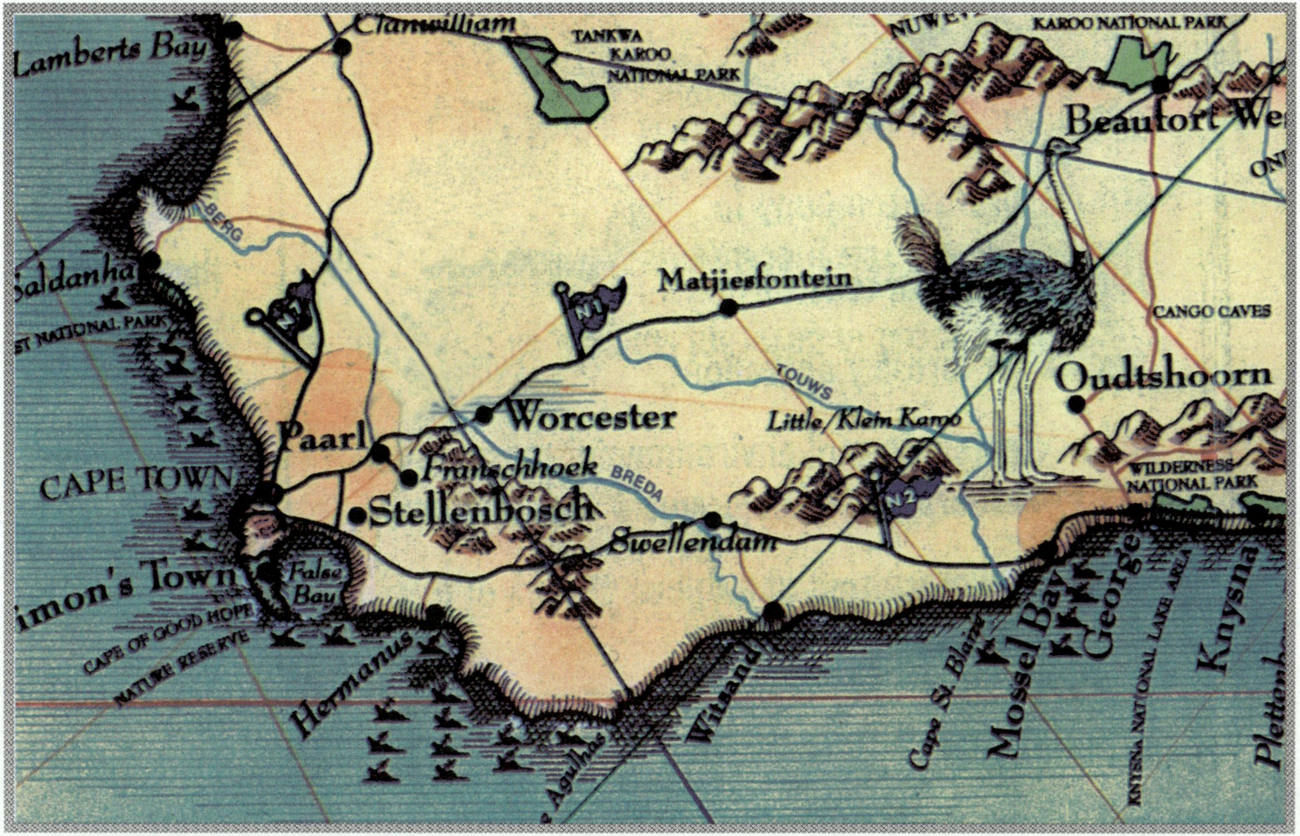

Map of Matjiesfontein and the Karoo

Windmill and reservoir at Matjiesfontein

CHAPTER XX

RENAISSANCE

'And then along came John' was the title of a popular song of the 'fifties but in this case it was not a John but a David - David Rawdon, who came along in 1968 on an heroic rescue mission. And if J.D. Logan was the creator of the village of Matjiesfontein, then David Rawdon could be said to have recreated it, and was perhaps the only person who could have achieved this.

Rawdon had hoped to become a horse-breeder after having done service in the South African Air Force as a rear gunner, but this ambition was thwarted by circumstance. Instead, together with his mother and his brother Graham, he established the small but elegant country hotel, Rawdons, in the Nottingham Road district. Then in 1958, David bought a portion of the farm Lanzerac at Stellenbosch including its lovely old Cape Dutch homestead, dilapidated, but with great potential.

David restored Lanzerac most meticulously, such that it became a country hotel of considerable charm and culinary fame.

For several years Rawdon had had the village of Matjiesfontein in his sights, without ever giving himself much hope of acquiring it. Then, having heard that the executors of J. D. Logan's estate were considering selling the hotel, he wrote to them offering to buy the entire village. His offer was initially refused. However, after months of negotiation his dream was finally realised and in 1968 he bought the whole village, consisting of thirty acres, twenty houses and cottages, the Masonic and Milner Hotels, the former school, the courthouse, town hall, store and post office, for a total sum of ninety thousand Rands. The use of the beautiful colonial homestead, Tweedside Lodge, was to be retained by the family until the death of the present head of the family, Major John Buist.

David Rawdon expected to spend three or four times the purchase price on restoration and renovation. Being as much a perfectionist in his own way as the creator of Matjesfontein, J.D. Logan, he is a painstaking stickler for detail. In many ways the neglected state of the village was an advantage, in that no-one had so much as attempted any renovations, which would in any case have to be removed and replaced. Rawdon stripped the buildings inside and out, replastering and painting. Preserving the shell intact yet recreating anything of original beauty he was able to uncover or discover from contemporary photographs, such as the papier-mâché mouldings above the door of the Milner Hotel, now the Lord Milner Hotel, he restored Matjiesfontein to its original splendour. The major renovations consisted in rebuilding the old store, which had been destroyed by fire, so that it once more became the double storey building it once was. This building now became the Coffee Shop. Rawdon also increased the number of bathrooms in the main hotel.

The Masonic Hotel, now renamed "Die Losieshuis", has become a charming old world lodging house. A building, possibly the old Village Hall, now known as "The Laird's Arms" is very reminiscent of an

English pub. The crowning glory is the Lord Milner itself with its superb original pine ceilings, grand staircase, sash windows, pillars and wide verandahs. The stone fountains in the forecourt play again as they did almost a century ago. And in the dining room – which retains its original "Elephant Quality" linoleum floor, and the beautiful chairs and tables dating from its inception, is a magnificent ornamental iron column which has its twin "somewhere in Buckingham Palace."

David Rawdon is an inveterate and well-informed collector of antiques and works of art. He found much of his present furniture in British antique shops, and transported this to Matjiesfontein, where it blends perfectly with what remains of the original furnishings. Among the superb Victorian pieces decorating the interior are the exquisite chandeliers which came from the home of the late Sir Abe Bailey.

The building that once served as the gas plant for the village has been turned into an enchanting small chapel.

David Rawdon's vision culminated in the celebration in 1984 of Matjiesfontein's centenary, when the village was en féte with staff and visitors, all clad in Victorian clothes. The festivities included a steam train, an army encampment, Scottish pipers, a commando, a cricket match, dances, grand luncheons and dinners, a performance by Elize Cawood of Olive Schreiner's works in The Courthouse and a recital by the Stellenbosch University Choir. At the opening ceremony, the grandson and great-granddaughter of the founder of Matjesfontein wore the court dresses worn at the coronation of Edward VII in 1901 by Jimmy and

Emma Logan.

Rawdon has established a museum which houses an extensive collection of Victoriana as well as some of the beautiful dresses that belonged to Emma Logan. It gives a fascinating picture of days long past. And one is amazed to see the forerunners of washing machines, vacuum cleaners and knife polishers on display. One can only guess at the possible uses of some of the other, stranger devices!

Perhaps a kilometre away from the Victorian village, on the other side of the tracks, are the small brick and iron cottages, built by the railway for its employees, and among the modern little houses are some much older cottages thought to date back to the original Matjesfontein, when the inhabitants still made reed mats for their livelihood. Today many of the hotel staff are housed there.

Yes, the magic is back. As one turns into Logan Street with its pretty Victorian cottages, the lamps that once were lit by gas, the lovely old filigree iron fences, the turreted Lord Milner Hotel, Union Jack flag flying, the pepper trees that David Rawdon planted and now are grown wide and tall, while all around the limitless Karoo, one steps back a century in time. Olive Schreiner referred to the 'curious and to me very attractive mixture of civilization and wild untamed freedom.' One can imagine that J. D. Logan, whose brooding portrait and massive personality still pervade, would delight again in his beloved Matjiesfontein.

Olive Schreiner's tree still stands, the air is as pure, the emptiness, the space are there. And at night the stars shine as brightly as they did on Jimmy and Emma Logan when they began their lifetime journey together.

APPENDIX I

THE JAMESON RAID

In order to retain control of the population, the government of the Transvaal Republic sought to impose severe franchise requirements on the "Uitlanders", or newly-arrived immigrants. Only after fourteen years residence, would an "Uitlander" be granted voting rights enabling him to vote for a candidate to the Volksraad, while a new burgher (citizen) must have reached the age of forty before he was allowed full voting rights, i.e. the ability to vote for the State President, or to stand as a candidate for the Raad.

With the sudden influx of about one hundred thousand new immigrants and roughly fifty thousand local African employees to the area, what was most urgently required was an efficient police force, an abundant water supply, proper sanitation enforced by effective sanitary regulations, and liquor licensing laws. None of these was provided, although the treasury was overflowing and taxes continued to rise. Dutch was the only medium of instruction allowed in the state schools. "Taxation without representation" would be an accurate description of the treatment meted out to the "Uitlanders".

The "Reform" initiative, which aimed principally at redressing the grievances of the "Uitlanders" in a more egalitarian society, gathered considerable momentum with the arrival in Johannesburg of the imperialistic attorney Charles Leonard. He had moved from Cape Town to the Transvaal Republic with the specific intention of promoting the cause of the "Uitlanders" and bringing about a more democratic and equitable political and socio-economic system in the Transvaal. To this end, he helped to establish the Transvaal National Union in 1892, to forward the cause of the "Uitlanders" – the controlling body of which was the Reform Committee.

The local mining houses, which wielded some influence in their own right, had generally been opposed to any form of agitation to bring about political and economic change, as this might threaten mining prosperity and be detrimental to the industry as a whole, quite apart from the possible damage it might cause to mine property.

However, by 1894 these companies were becoming increasingly irked by heavy taxation and maladministration by the Volksraad. Further, surface mining was by now increasingly giving way to deep-level mining for which dynamite was a prerequisite, dynamite which could only be obtained at prohibitive cost due to a monopoly granted by the government. This monopoly and others, combined with extremely high tariffs for, inter alia, transport of coal and mining machinery, served to escalate working costs to uneconomical levels. A new, more efficient Volksraad was badly needed.

All this gave rise to a conspiracy to topple Kruger's government, and it was believed that the mere threat of an armed uprising would be sufficient to achieve this. A bloodless revolution was envisaged.

The conspiracy had the tacit backing of at least some of the local mining houses. An indication of their support was the fact that representatives of both Rhodes' Consolidated Goldfields of South Africa and the Wernher Beit group had by now joined the "Uitlander" Committee.

Cecil John Rhodes had two main agendas, one revolving around the interests of his mining company while the other, of far greater magnitude and unbeknown to most, centred on his overriding desire to bring about an African Federation under the control of the British Government.

By the middle of 1895 a rising seemed certain; what was uncertain was under which flag, the Union Jack or the "Vierkleur" (the flag of the Transvaal Republic), the rising would take place.

In retrospect an armed uprising could hardly be justified. Time was on the side of the "Uitlanders". Paul Kruger would in the foreseeable future have been outvoted and the "Uitlander" grievances renegotiated on more favourable terms.

Even among his own people, Kruger was by no means universally popular, and nor was his Volksraad. Leading figures such as Eugene Marais, Ewald Esselen, Carl Jeppe and Louis Botha were among his severest critics. He had appointed Dutch officials from Holland to many key positions in his government, and this caused widespread resentment.

On the other hand, time was not on Rhodes' side. He had to bring about a rising before the more moderate "Uitlanders" were able to negotiate an agreement with Kruger or form an "Uitlander" republic independent of Britain, perhaps with the support of another colonial power such as Germany. Yet at the same time he had to exercise great care and discretion. Had the direct involvement of the British South Africa Company and the complicity of the British Government in the conspiracy been known, much popular sympathy with the movement would have been lost.

In his book, Impressions of South Africa, published in 1897, James Bryce, a visitor in Johannesburg just before the Raid, wrote:

"Never before was there, except on the stage, so open a conspiracy. Two-thirds of the action went on before the public. The visitor had hardly installed himself in a hotel in Pretoria before people began to tell him that an insurrection was imminent, that Maxim guns were hidden and would be shown to him if he cared to see them ... In Johannesburg little else was talked of, not in dark corners, but at the club where everybody lunches, and between the acts at the play!"

Another equally ardent imperialist was the High Commissioner, Sir Henry Loch. He, with Jameson and Rhodes, had been heavily involved in the plot. Rhodes formed a company, New Concessions, which his brother Frank used to finance the purchase of arms and ammunition for the rising. In 1894 Rhodes, in the name of the British South Africa Company, or the Charter Company as it was otherwise known, obtained control of a strip of land along the border of the Bechuanaland Protectorate, 6000 square miles in extent. This acquisition was made ostensibly to enable Rhodes to extend the railway from Mafeking to Bulawayo, but in reality it gave him the opportunity to establish a secret base camp at Pitsani, from which he could invade the Transvaal should the "Uitlander" uprising take place.

And what of the man, Leander Starr Jameson, whose name will forever be inextricably linked with the Raid? One description portrays him as "a swashbuckling sidekick of Rhodes", while another remarks on his "bouncing self-confidence".

Born in Scotland in 1853, Jameson was the 11th and last child of Robert and Christian Jameson. After an initial schooling in Scotland, he went on to receive his B.S. and M.D. degrees at the University College in London and then qualified for membership of the Royal College of Surgeons. To all intents and purposes, a brilliant future awaited him in London. But in 1876 he forsook London, opting instead for a share in a general practice in the remote town of Kimberley, which at that time formed part of the Cape Colony.

The fact that his elder brother was living there may have influenced him in his decision; otherwise he may simply have given full rein to his joyous sense of adventure. Jameson arrived at Kimberley in 1878 at the age of 25, soon becoming a highly respected and very popular doctor. His career in the country town was meteoric; in 1879 he was appointed one of Kimberley's three medical consultants. It was at Kimberley that Jameson met Rhodes and became a close friend. They were the same age and Jameson soon became more and more involved in Rhodes' visions and plans, so much so that by 1890 he was the Administrator of Mashonaland and of one mind with Rhodes in planning to bring the Transvaal under British rule.

Pitsani was the nearest base from which a relief attack on Johannesburg could be mounted. It was agreed that Jameson was to train and mount a force of 1500 men to come to the aid of the "Uitlanders", with some 3000 rifles. To this end the Reform Committee furnished Jameson with a letter signed by Charles Leonard, Frank Rhodes, George Farrar and Lionel

Phillips, outlining the "Uitlander" grievances, foretelling an uprising and calling on Jameson to come to the rescue of "... thousands of unarmed men, women and children of our race ... at the mercy of well-armed boers." This letter was undated so that an appropriate date could be inserted later, to make it seem an immediate appeal.

However, by mid-December 1895, enthusiasm for an uprising had waned and much of the support had dwindled. In Johannesburg it became apparent that far fewer men were prepared to take up arms, than the 3000 that had originally been anticipated. So that, after many coded telegrams to and from Cape Town, Johannesburg and London, from Rhodes, from Sir Hercules Robinson the newly-appointed High Commissioner, from the Colonial Office, the eventual conclusion reached by the "Uitlander" leaders was that the Raid should be postponed or cancelled. This decision was arrived at notwithstanding a reference to the projected Raid in a message on December the 18th from the then Colonial Secretary, Joseph Chamberlain, to Robert Meade, then Permanent under-secretary to the Colonial Office, reading as follows, "Now as to the Transvaal ... it seems that either it (the Raid) should come at once or be postponed for a year or two at least."

However, Jameson was still under the impression that the planned uprising for Saturday December the 28th 1895 would go ahead as planned. By the end of November he had mustered a force of not 1500, but 450 men, including 250 of the Mashonaland Mounted Police, with horses, mules, six Maxim and two Field Guns. The policemen, together with their horses, mules and guns, had been diverted from the protection of the construction of the railway line to Bulawayo, which was their official duty.

Sir John Willoughby, commander of the volunteer regiment, the Rhodesia Horse, was appointed Jameson's Chief-of-Staff. This company, numbering some 1000 men scattered throughout Matabeleland, was to be put in a state of readiness while Willoughby left for Pitsani on December the 9th 1895.

Frank Rhodes had telegraphed Jameson on December the 7th to inform him that the "polo tournament" had been postponed, but Jameson, already nervous that suspicion had been aroused, insisted that there should be no delay.

Although Cecil Rhodes was being urged to halt the uprising, he nevertheless sent messages to Jameson on December the 23rd and the 24th advising that the rising would definitely take place on December the 28th – indeed, his words on December the 24th were, "You must not move before Saturday night; we are feeling confident it will take place on Saturday night."

It was only on December the 26th that Jameson was sent a coded message from his brother Sam in Johannesburg on behalf of the leaders of the Reform Committee, telling him not to move until so instructed. He also received messages from Cape Town exhorting him not to move and to be patient until the 6th of January 1896. To Jameson, the delay was devastating. Keyed up as he was to fever pitch after weeks and months of planning, the ever-temperamental and impulsive Jameson replied on December the 28th, "Unless I hear definitely to the contrary, I shall leave tomorrow evening and carry into effect my second telegram of yesterday to you."

His attitude caused consternation and alarm in Johannesburg. John Hays Hammond, whom Jameson regarded as one of the more courageous leaders, had telegraphed him on December the 27th to state, "I absolutely condemn further developments at present."

Early on the Sunday morning of the 29th, Jameson had received a Reuters report that had appeared in Cape newspapers the previous day concerning warlike preparations in Johannesburg and telling of the mustering of Kruger's commandos. He had planned, together with the Johannesburg leaders of the uprising, that he should ride into the Transvaal immediately, should their plans become known. This arrangement was denied by the leaders afterwards. Perhaps it had merely been a suggestion during the planning stages. For Jameson, the report provided further justification for his actions.

Despite the verbal messages Jameson received from Johannesburg on the 28th brought by Captain Holden on horseback, and on the 29th by Major Heaney, who arrived by train to explain that the "Uitlanders" were disorganised and unmotivated, lacking arms and being at odds over the flag question, Jameson decided to ride into Johannesburg immediately.

Accordingly he paraded his men that afternoon and at 6.30 p.m. began the long ride to Johannesburg, being joined at Malmani by 122 men of the Bechuanaland Border Police from Mafeking.

Meanwhile Rhodes was at last persuaded that there would be no uprising – and he decided to abandon the plan. He even went so far as to tell Sir Graham Bower, the Imperial Secretary, on the evening of the 28th of December at Groote Schuur, that the revolution "... had fizzled out like a damp squib." He seemed, to Bowen, to be quite relieved that the Raid had not commenced, instead talking with enthusiasm of his plans for Rhodesia. He was also confident that Jameson would wait at Pitsani until he was told to move.

A prerequisite for a successful uprising had to be a degree of secrecy. In this instance Kruger and his cabinet were by now aware of virtually every move the Reformers made; the priceless advantage of secrecy had been lost.

Paul Kruger seemed to have been content to play "a waiting game" at this juncture. His words in this regard reportedly were:

"If you want to kill a tortoise, wait until it sticks its head out of its shell, then cut it off."

Worse was to come for the Reformers. Although Jameson had sent men ahead to cut all the telegraph wires north and south of Mafeking to and from Pitsani and Zeerust and to Pretoria in anticipation of the Raid, only the line to the South was in fact severed; either the line to Pretoria was overlooked, or, as legend would have it, the man detailed to cut it was so intoxicated that he mistook farm fence wires for the telegraph wires and cut and buried them instead! In effect, this meant that Kruger was able to follow Jameson's every move.

Militating still further against any slender chances of success the Raid may have had, was the fact that rifles sent to Johannesburg for use by the Reformers had not yet been unpacked and cleaned of protective grease.

It was known to the Reform leaders that Kruger's armoury was normally guarded by only six men at night in the usually quiet town of Pretoria. Part of the plan for the uprising was to overpower the guards and make off with the guns in the armoury. However, the timing of the attack was unfortunate; being Christmas, the town was bristling with thousands of Kruger's supporters, who were there for Nagmaal. There was no possibility of success and this plan had to be abandoned.

The supplies of food, fodder and fresh horses which were to have been cached at intervals along the route proved to be inadequate for the force of about 510 mounted men Jameson ultimately commanded. The two days Jameson had optimistically calculated he needed for the journey, became four.

Some of Kruger's commandos had followed Jameson's force almost from the outset. However, they possessed neither field- nor machine guns and Jameson's force was able to hold them at bay until they reached the outskirts of Krugersdorp. Alarmed by this turn of events, Jameson sent a message to Johannesburg reporting that his force had been involved in only two harmless scrimmages, but would be glad of an escort of 200 men at Krugersdorp to accompany the column to Johannesburg.

The expected escort never materialised. Worse, he was summarily informed that the only route his force could take was directly through Krugersdorp itself. Willoughby was firmly opposed to this route, but was overruled by Jameson. As the column approached Krugersdorp, it was discovered that a store of food and fodder cached for the troops some seven miles outside the town had been severely depleted, while the road ahead was flanked by Boer forces. Jameson was forced to retreat and strike camp after a skirmish costing him some 30 dead and wounded. At daybreak he sought another route southwards, with the commandos in hot pursuit. At 8 a.m. the British Agent's messenger and J.J. Lace caught up with the Raiders. They informed Jameson that the High Commissioner had given an order forbidding British subjects in Johannesburg from giving Jameson any assistance and that "Uitlander" leaders in the city were obeying the order; Jameson was advised to return to the border.

Soon after this dispiriting news, Jameson and his force reached the farm Vlakfontein. The way ahead was blocked by the kopje Doornkop and by commandos who held a low cliff on the right, while the commandos to the rear were closing in. His men put up a brief fight until the machine guns jammed, for lack of water to cool them. Then, outnumbered, outmanoeuvred, exhausted and hungry, they accepted defeat. A white apron together with bedsheets appropriated from one of the maids on the farm was tied to a wagon whipstock and hoisted through the roof of one of the farm outbuildings in a gesture of defeat. Seventeen Raiders had been killed and fifty-five were injured. General P.A. Cronje received their surrender graciously. A weeping Jameson was taken, with his officers, by cart to Pretoria, with his men following on horseback. On arrival they were all gaoled, yet their treatment at the hands of the Boers authorities was kindly. The men were disarmed and fed and the wounded taken to Krugersdorp hospital. Their horses were taken and their baggage and personal effects seized. Disastrously for the backers of the Raid and the "Uitlanders", telegrams in code from both Rhodes in Cape Town and the conspirators in Johannesburg, together with the code book itself, were found in Major Robert White's black tin box!

It was only on the afternoon of Monday the 31st of December that the news of Jameson's invasion of the Transvaal reached the Johannesburg leaders of the conspiracy. A telegraph from Mafeking reading "The contractor has started on the earthworks with seven hundred boys: hopes to reach terminus on Wednesday" left them in no doubt that despite all their attempts to call off the Raid, Jameson had indeed gone ahead.

In a state of great consternation and apprehension, the Reform Committee numbering about sixty, which had spearheaded the "Uitlander" rebellion, declared that it had no knowledge of Jameson's Raid; it pledged further that it was bound to uphold law and order in the Transvaal Republic. In spite of "Uitlander" recruiting drives, drilling, the digging of trenches and handing-out of rifles, any acts of violence had been studiously avoided.

When news of Jameson's defeat was received, the Reform Committee hastened to comply with the Government's terms of unconditional surrender and disarmament, in the hope that the High Commissioner would be able to come to their assistance.

The Volksraad already knew who the members of the Reform Committee were; in a naive earlier attempt to establish its credibility and status in good faith, it had supplied the Boer administration with a full list of its members!

On January the 9th President Kruger promised to pardon all those who gave up arms against the Transvaal Republic, with the exception of the leaders and instigators of the revolt. By nightfall, sixty-four members of the reform committee had been rounded up and jailed. Four of the leaders were condemned to death, but their sentences were later commuted to heavy fines; the remainder receiving varying terms in gaol or fines. The thirty-six officers arrested were given the choice of abstaining from politics for fifteen years or going into exile, a number of the Raiders being sent to England on January the 25th for trial, with the fate of the rank-and-file to be decided by the British Government. Jameson and Willoughby were each sentenced to fifteen months' imprisonment in Holloway gaol.

Meanwhile Rhodes, still in Cape Town, appeared to have fallen into the grip of inertia. It seems incredible that although he eventually realised that the plan to overthrow Kruger could not possibly succeed and must be abandoned, he made no attempt to communicate directly with Jameson in an attempt to avert impending disaster. Nor indeed, when he heard that Jameson had crossed the border into the Transvaal, did he make any effort to stop him before the situation worsened. Was he in his heart of hearts hoping against hope, that Jameson would somehow succeed against all odds? When asked by W.P. Schreiner why he was doing nothing to stop Jameson in his folly, he replied simply:

"Poor old Jameson. Twenty years we have been friends, and now he goes in and ruins me. I cannot hinder him. I cannot go and destroy him."

When Rhodes heard of Jameson's surrender, he immediately resigned as Prime Minister of the Cape Colony. Thereafter, he tried to make peace with the Afrikaner Bond; J.H. Hofmeyr advised him to withdraw from politics and leave the Cape Colony for a few years. However, Rhodes was by now obsessed with saving the Charter Company he had founded and hurried to England in an attempt to retrieve the situation. Arriving in London on February the 3rd, he was called upon to testify before the English Parliament, as to his part in the Raid. He disavowed any complicity the British Government may have had in the conspiracy and was allowed to return to his adopted homeland a free man.

The Raid, ill-conceived, poorly planned and badly executed as it was, only served to exacerbate and intensify the mutual distrust between Boer and Briton at a critical time. The Boers were by now convinced that Britain intended to seize and annex the Boer republics when the moment was ripe and began to prepare for war.

Kruger was hailed as the hero and the champion of the Boer republics and was returned to power in the 1898 elections with an overwhelming majority.

General Jan Christiaan Smuts was in 1906 to refer to the Raid as the real declaration of war between the Afrikaner nation and Britain.

The old homestead at Vlakfontein where Jameson hid from Boer forces

The Old Barn at Vlakfontein, largest in the ZAR, where Hendrik Brink imprisoned the British officers for trespassing

The woman whose apron and bedsheets were used by Jameson and his men as a flag of surrender

Hendrik Brink - 'Lord of Vlakfontein'

Vlakfontein homestead after the 1948 tornado had blown the thatched roof away

Jameson Raid Monument after the plinth had been knocked down by the 1948 tornado

Jameson's Monument restored after the ravages of the 1948 tornado
(All photographs of Vlakfontein by courtesy of Marthinus van Bart)

The original Court House in Matjesfontein, adjacent to the old School House

APPENDIX II

LOGAN'S LITIGATION

JIMMY LOGAN, LEGENDARY LITIGANT AND 'LAIRD OF MATJESFONTEIN'
by Louis Rood
(From De Rebus; December 1997 issue):

"Much may be made of a Scotchman if he be caught young"
(Dr. Samuel Johnson 1709 – 1784)

'Litigation is not for the fainthearted. Most people, sensibly, tend to avoid the cold reality of the courtroom. But, occasionally, one comes across an individual who relishes using the weapons the law provides to achieve his ends ...

Probably the most prolific litigant that South Africa has seen and certainly the most colourful was the extraordinary entrepreneur, Jimmy Logan ...

In 1894 Logan stood as a Progressive in the Worcester constituency and was elected to the Cape Legislative Assembly. His name began appearing with increasing frequency in the law reports. South Africa was a land of opportunity and an ambition such as that of Logan could not be contained. Inevitably toes were trampled upon ...

In 1889 Logan was sued by the formidable Sir Alfred Beit. A friend and associate of Rhodes, Beit had already amassed a vast fortune. He had established the British South Africa Chartered Company in 1888 and extended his phenomenal diamond acquisitions to the

Witwatersrand goldfields. Beit's action for the delivery of shares in the Worcester Exploration and Gold Mining Company, alternatively for damages, was heard in the Griqualand High Court by Judge President Laurence and Judge Cole. The company had been registered by Logan the previous year. It is an indication of the bold acumen of Logan, not only that he would venture into the mining industry from his base in the Cape, but that a seasoned speculator like Beit could be persuaded to invest in the enterprise. Logan himself gave evidence of discussions held "in front of Barnato's Bar" in Kimberley. Disputes of fact resulted in Beit achieving partial success with Logan ordered to bear the costs (Beit v Logan 1884 GHC 458) ...

Logan did not take defeat lying down. He appealed. Two months later Chief Justice Lord de Villiers, sitting with Judges Buchanan and Smith heard the appeal. Logan was represented by James Rose-Innes and Malcolm Searle. Beit by Schreiner and Watermeyer. Logan succeeded with costs (Logan v Beit 1890 SC 197) ...

Logan had a keen eye for a business opportunity. In 1885 the first official train from Cape Town arrived in Kimberley with the opening of the railway line. Logan's licence permitted him to sell liquor by retail at the Kimberley railways station "within a reasonable time before and after the arrival or departure of any train at such station". His contract with the railways stipulated that he should not be permitted to open his premises on Sundays 'for longer than one hour before arrival and after departure of trains'. To the outrage of competing bars, like that of the Gladstone Hotel opposite the station, Logan proceeded to sell liquor on

Sundays and during the permitted hours to patrons, none of whom even pretended to be passengers on any train. He was convicted by the magistrate for selling liquor on a Sunday, a contravention of the Liquor Licensing Amendment Act 44 of 1885. Logan appealed. Judge President Laurence upheld the conviction, but his plugging of the loophole exploited by Logan is anything but convincing. He concluded that:

"Persons in the position of the appellant are entitled to sell liquor on weekdays to any person, but on Sundays only to persons actually arriving or departing by train" (R v Logan 1891 GHC) ...

But even Logan's love of cricket was not without acrimony. He had promised £500 in support of the first South African team to tour England in 1894 under H.H. Carstens, a lawyer who had previously also captained South Africa in its first rugby test in 1891. Carstens' team was the first from South Africa to play at Lord's where they beat a team captained by the legendary W.G. Grace. Logan withdrew his offer when the manager of his choice was not selected ...

In 1892 Logan launched an action for the repayment of £750 lent by him to W.W. Read – captain of the first English cricket team of 1891/1892 to tour South Africa which won the only test played at Cape Town by an innings and 189 runs – and Edwin Ash, the secretary of the team. Read had previously led England on a tour of Australia. The defendants dug themselves in, raising an exception, which succeeded with costs (Logan v Read and Ash 1892 S/C514) Spurred on the defendants moved to strike out the action. This time they failed with costs ... in the cause. (Logan v Read and Ash 1893 S/C 50) Logan had both defendants arrested as they were on the point of departing for England, compelling them to put up security for his claims ...

The contest came to trial in June 1893. Logan stood his ground in the witness box. He testified:

"I saw Read at a cricket match in Edinburgh. He asked me whether it was to be peace or war. And I replied if he meant by war that I intended to get my money, there would be war."

The courts were becoming Logan's own turf and this was a war he was to win. Logan's evidence was accepted and he took Judgement with costs (Logan v Read and Ash 1893 CTR 201) ...

Logan also had dealings with the equally flamboyant Barney Barnato, founder of the Johannesburg Consolidated Investment Company. Barnato died after falling overboard on a voyage to England in 1897. Logan sued Barnato's executor, attorney E.T. Solomon £4.350.00 with interest for shares bought by him for Barnato. He gave evidence of the transaction and discussions he had with Barnato at the Royal Hotel at Cape Town. They had been in partnership together on the Kimberley Stock Exchange. Logan was granted leave to take evidence from Barnato's nephew Solly Joel in London (Logan v Barnato's estate 1899 CTR 31). Fellow member of Parliament George Palmer testified:

"I certainly think Mr Barnato's mind was unhinged at that time and he became gradually worse until the steamer sailed."

Granting absolution from the instance because of lack of written records of the alleged transaction, Chief Justice De Villiers commented:

"It seems that Mr Logan has had a great many transactions of this nature but his chief business is that of commerce; this speculation in shares seems to be a kind of by-play on his part". (Logan v Barnato's executors 1893 CTR 486) ...

During the Anglo-Boer War of 1899-1902, Matjiesfontein became the headquarters of the Cape Command with 12,000 troops camped around the village. The turret of Logan's Milner Hotel was used as a lookout post, while the hotel became a military hospital. Logan raised his own mounted corps for service in the field, was twice wounded and mentioned in despatches ...

This loyalty to the Crown did not deter Logan from litigating against the Colonial Government. In June 1900 he successfully interdicted the railways from advertising for contracts for its refreshment rooms and bookstalls until expiration in 1902 of Logan's five year contract giving him exclusive right of operating bookstalls, refreshment rooms and bars on the railway stations in question. (Logan & Co Ltd v Colonial Government 1900 CTR 379) ...

In February 1901 Logan moved for a declaratory order that he was not obliged to pay rent to the Government for the refreshment room bookstall and bar at Warrenton station for the period that it was occupied by the Boer forces, from October 1899 to May 1900 when the leased property could not be used by him. Schreiner QC for the Colonial Government, clothed himself in imperialist outrage:

"It is monstrous that the court should be asked to recognise the fact that parts of this colony had been conquered!"

Drawing on wartime precedent the court ordered Logan to pay the rental and the costs (Logan & Co. Ltd., v Colonial Government 1901 CTR 84) ...

A few weeks later the same parties were in court, again for a declaration of rights, this time arising from the expropriation of a portion of Logan's farm known as De Draai at Touws River. Logan succeeded with costs and was declared entitled to compensation for the expropriation. This was one of the earliest cases in which photographs of the locality were taken and submitted in evidence. Logan asked for, but was not awarded the costs of such photographs. (Logan v Colonial Government 1901 CTR 114) ...

Stung by Logan's persistence, the government applied for and was granted leave to appeal to the Privy Council (Logan v Colonial Government 1901 CTR 216) ...

Logan struck back. He moved for an interdict to restrain the Cape Railways from using the land expropriated until its appeal to the Privy Council had been heard. Logan won his order with costs to stand over until the decision of the Privy Council had been given (Logan v Colonial Government 1901 CTR 468) ...

The Law Lords of the Privy Council found for Logan and dismissed the appeal. The calculation of compensation was referred to arbitrators and in May 1904 the award by the arbitrators to Logan of £1,170.00 with costs was made an order of court. (Logan v Colonial Government 1904 CTR 341) ...

The pugnacious nature of Logan when it came to litigation could be carried to extremes. A few years later the government was compelled to seek the court's approval to rectify the deed of transfer of the land expropriated because of a misdescription. Counsel alleged that it was Logan's fault that the error had occurred, but that "he had ignored their requests for a correct transfer". The order was granted with costs (Colonial Government v Logan 1908 CTR 1056) ...

There was a further sequel to this saga. Logan brought an action for damages against the Cape government for the pollution of the Touws River running through his farm De Draai. The railways had provided housing for its employees on the land expropriated and created a "location on which are erected many huts". Night soil and noxious refuse deposited on the banks of the river were endangering the health of the occupants of Logan's farm. Experts were called, including Dr. P.D. Hahn, Professor of Chemistry at the SA College. A tender of £500 was made, but true to form, spurned by Logan. That was a calculated risk, which failed. Logan obtained judgement for only the amount of the tender and costs up to the date it was made. He had to bear the later costs. (Logan v Colonial Government 1910 CTR 225) ...

The economic slump after the Boer War affected Logan's extensive Commercial interests. One finds him settling with one of his debtors, a hotel keeper (Logan v Abrahamson 1905 CTR 239) and then sequestrating him (Logan v Abrahamson 1905 CTR 375). He then urgently applied for a provisional trustee to be appointed in the insolvent estate of Henry Hewitt to keep the Commercial Hotel in Worcester operating. (Ex parte Logan and another 1909 CTR 851) ...

He became embroiled in an undignified squabble with the Laingsburg School Board, claiming a lien over certain woodwork implements and school furniture and demanding storage of £1.00 per month. Although Logan succeeded before the resident magistrate, the School Board won its appeal and Logan was ordered to pay costs. (Laingsburg School Board v Logan 1910 CTR 309) ...

In June 1907 his company James D. Logan and Co. Ltd. was placed in voluntary liquidation by him. The liquidator Harry Hands was sued for £18,083 in damages because Poole's Hotel in Queen Victoria Street, Cape Town, leased for twenty years to the company had been partially demolished. Pooles had been a popular city watering hole. (Cecil Rhodes had stayed there) but became somewhat dilapidated. The judge concluded that the building had been pulled down ...

"... because there was a scheme in the mind of Mr Logan who was manager of the company to develop this place into a first class modern hotel."

The scheme failed and so did the liquidator's defence. He was ordered to pay the costs. (Hutchinson v Logan and Co. Ltd.1908 CTR 116) ...

The Law Reports reveal other indications of Logan's increasingly troubled business affairs. He was reduced to bringing an application to set aside a default judgement taken against him. Although the summons was served on his private secretary, H.C. Hoy, it was not brought to his attention (Logan v Spence 1908 CTR 254). Logan's counsel thereafter applied for his evidence to be taken on commission as he was in London. The court was told that:

"Mr Logan said before he left that he would fight the case to a finish". (Logan v Spence 1908 CTR 436) ...

Default judgement was also taken against Logan in his capacity as a surety for Brandon Kirby who leased the Round House above Camps Bay but had failed to pay rent for six months. (Cape Town Council v Logan 1908 CTR 177). A writ was issued and Logan now applied to set it aside to reopen the case and to join Kirby as a co-defendent. Despite protests that "Mr Logan had been entirely and grossly negligent in the case from start to finish" he was granted his orders. (Logan and another v Cape Town Council 1908 CTR 262). Logan put up the security required but neither he nor Kirby then entered appearance. The irate Town Council then applied afresh for default judgement against Logan only, for payment of the security and costs and it was so ordered. (Cape Town Council v Logan and another 1908 CTR 307) ...

Jimmy Logan's lack of attention to detail of his own affairs was again illustrated when he applied for the deed of transfer of the Masonic Hotel in Beaufort West to be amended to reflect himself as owner, and not his company in liquidation. He succeeded, saving the property from the clutches of creditors. Judge Buchanan ambiguously remarked "Logan and Logan and Co Ltd. seem to have been very much mixed up in this matter" and ordered him to bear the costs. (Logan v Treasurer General and Others 1908 CTR 976) ...

The Laird, however, was far from a spent force politically. He had been a member of the Upper House for the Northwest Cape since 1898. In September 1907 he held the balance of power and despite various parliamentary maneouvres to gain approval of the Estimates Bill this was effectively blocked by Logan. This deadlock eventually compelled Prime Minister Jameson to dissolve both Houses of Parliament. A general election followed and Merriman became Prime Minister in February 1908 ...

Now in his fifties, Logan's forays into court became rarer. In 1912 he obtained provisional sentence on a dishonoured cheque and judgement for other debts totalling £2,663.00 (Logan v Bishop 1912 WR 316). In 1914 he brought an application putting the respondents to terms in a pending action. An affidavit stated that Logan had been advised by his doctors to go to Europe. The court had little sympathy ...

"The whole of the application was premature and unnecessary. It would be refused with costs." (Logan v le Fleur and Others 1914 WR 324) ...

Logan's health compelled him to return to Scotland but he was drawn back to his beloved Matjiesfontein where he died on 30 July 1920. A few months later his former tenant, Olive Schreiner, also passed away ...

Some years later Jimmy Logan lined the purses of his attorneys one final time. In 1935 his son, James in his capacity as administrator of Logan's estate – having been so appointed on the death of the previous adminstrator, Sir James Sivewright – applied for authority to pass transfer of certain land in Loganda Township. Logan's will was interpreted to permit this and it was authorised. (Estate Logan v Registrar of Deeds 1935 CP.D 42) ...

Logan and Sivewright can truly be numbered high among those of Scottish descent who made their mark in Southern Africa. This clan of pioneers includes Andrew Geddes Bain, John Fairbairn, Dr Leander Starr Jameson, Dr John Philip, Dr James Barry, Thomas Pringle and Dr David Livingstone ...

In 1969 the slumbering village of Matjiesfontein was bought and superbly restored to its former

Victorian charm by David Rawdon. Overnight guests of the Lord Milner Hotel are now awakened for breakfast by the bugle call for reveille. Logan's grandson Major Buist still lives in the village, which is a national monument. In Touws River the tradition of roadside hospitality continues in the Loganda Hotel. But the dust has long since settled on the courtroom jousts of the feisty and fearless Jimmy Logan.'

Louis Rood BA LLB (UCT) is an attorney at Fairbridge Arderne and Lawton in Cape Town. This article has been reproduced in abridged form with his kind permission.

APPENDIX III

HISTORICAL DOCUMENTS

J.D. Logan's official coat of arms

THE BLACK WATCH AT MAGERSFONTEIN

(by one who was there)

– December 11th, 1899.

Tell you a tale of the battle!
Well, there is not much to tell,
Nine hundred went to the slaughter,
And nigh on four hundred fell.

Wire and the Mauser rifle,
Thirst and the burning sun,
Knocked us down by the hundred,
Ere the long day was done.

Wet was the night, cold and dreary,
Chilled were the men to the bone,
Bivouacked there in the open,
Thinking perhaps of their home.

Midnight they came round to wake us,
Forming us up in the dark,
Officers whispered their orders,
Never a light or a spark.

Onward we went till the morning
Dawned in the East, grey and drear,
While in the front of us looming,
The kopjes bold outline showed clear.

Away on the left of the kopjes
We noticed a light burning bright,
And just as the column had halted,
It suddenly vanished from sight.

Then ere we knew what had happened,
Two shots on our left ringing out,
To the Boers in their trenches gave signal,
And rifle balls answered our shout.

Someone yelled "Charge!" and we started
Rose up and rushed out in fire,
Meaning to give them the bayonet,
But checked and stopped by the wire.

Bullets and shells ne'er appalled us,
Trenches nor boulder strewn hill,
But just a few yards of wire fencing,
Brought us, nonplussed, standing still.

"Over the wire men, or through it,
Drive the charge home to the hilt!!!"
Vain were the struggles and climbing,
Barbs sticking deep thro' the kilt.

Strong grows the light of the morning,
We halted, the lead on us rained,
Still we remained there before them,
Holding the ground we had gained.

"Down on the face, men - seek cover!"
Nothing could live in that fire,
"Off to the right, men, to flank them!
Forward! Lie down men! Retire!"

Then we turned back and we cursed them,
Macfarlane's dead form stood erect,
Volley on volley we gave them,
Until their fierce fire was checked.

Then our brave Adjutant rallied
Remnants of different Corps,
Some of the Black Watch and Argyles,
And some of the gallant Seaforths.

All day long in the same position,
Watching our own shells burst,
Lying with dead men and wounded,
Lips swollen blue-black with thirst.

Not thirty yards from the trenches,
Brave General Wauchope lay dead,
Our Colonel, too, lay beside him,
Their lives by the Boer bullets sped.

Such was the day for our regiment,
Dread the revenge we will take,
Dearly we paid for the blunder,
A drawingroom General's mistake.

Where was the Guard's "gallant" General;
Three miles in our rear out of sight,
No one to issue us orders,
Men doing what they thought was right.

Not a man knew when we started
What we were going to do,
Take up or rush a position,
Were the Boers many or few.

Had they retired! Were they coming!
Had they slunk off in the night!
Should we attack in the darkness!
Or wait to attack in the daylight!

Why weren't we told of the trenches!
Why weren't we told of the wire!
Why attack in the quarter column!
May Tommy Atkins enquire!

Why were no scouts sent forward!
Why were no scouts on our flank!
Why were we marched up in column!
Who made the mistake! Give his rank.

Do they know his name in Old England!
Do they know his incompetence yet!
Tommy has learned to his sorrow,
Any Tommy will never forget.

Nigh on eight hundred our losses,
English and Irish and Scotch,
Half of them fell in one regiment!
God help the noble Black Watch.

Such is the tale of the battle,
It's easy for me now to tell,
But nine hundred men in a death trap,
And nearly four hundred fell!!!

The poem was taken down by a Private (Volunteer Company) at the dictation of one of the Black Watch while they were together in the Convalescent Camp at De Aar.

[illegible]

GOVERNMENT HOUSE,
CAPE TOWN.

November 24 .. 1899

Dear Sir.

I am engaged with others here in carrying out Red Cross work for the benefit of sick and wounded in the present war

It is desired to form in connection with the Head Centre in Cape Town - which embraces the Good Hope Society - the St. John Ambl. Association and the British Red Cross Society - Agencies at the places on the Railway through which the sick and wounded will pass from the front to the Base Hospitals and Wynberg or who may be detained as patients ~~at the~~ in Hospital - with a view to affording them comforts - at such places.

It is essential however that such aid should be rendered only under arrangements approved by the Local, Military Medical Authorities and as a Branch of the Red Cross work organised here.

I shall be glad therefore to receive the names of a small number of ladies and gentlemen say not exceeding 6. who would form themselves into a local Red Cross Committee. who will work in aid of the Sick and Wounded under the above Conditions. and one who will act as correspondent the Head Centre. and as an Agent for receiving and distributing stores sent up from here.

An early answer would be much appreciated.

I am

Yours faithfully

Annie E. Hanbury Williams

To

The Honble. J. D. Logan.

HOTELS
St Enoch Station, Glasgow
Dumfries & Ayr.
Refreshment Rooms
St Enoch Station, Glasgow
Princes Pier Station Greenock
Kilmarnock Ayr & Dumfries
Manager

St Enoch Station Hotel
Glasgow Sep. 12th 189[illegible]

My Darling Tillie! I have just dropped in here on passing to drop you a few lines as it will be my only chance to do so to catch the mail. I am sorry to say I am not much better and shall only be too pleased when I see dear old Metropolis

again. I hope this will reach you in better health than what you were when I got your last letter. W. Hogg. Dad. Finlayson. Clark Jimmie and myself have been through the highlands and they have all enjoyed it very much. Fancy we were in Oban the same time this year as we were last year when the Regatta was. We had a wretched do. Coming down the Canal both Finlayson and myself were very seedy. I am trying to finish my business here today

and your own party in
Edinburgh tomorrow
they have gone down
the Clyde. I have a
lot to do so as to get
ready to sail with the Scot
but am determined to
come if I am well
whether my business is
finished or not.

I will write you a
long letter next mail
and give you all the
news. So kindly excuse
this short note. It is
the only short letter I
have sent you Annie
Eleft.

Good Bye my
darling little wife until
we meet again which
I hope will be soon
and with all my
love & kisses

Believe me
Your Ever true
Loving Dadda

God bless you —
Kindest regards to all
+ + + + + + +

Genl. F.W.F. Walker
29.11.99.
re accommodation
for wounded at M[illegible]

The Castle
Capetown.
Nov. 29th/99.

Dear Sir,

In answer to your letter to Sir Redvers Buller with regard to your very kind offer of 5 villas at Matjesfontein for the use of the wounded on their way down, I beg to thank you most heartily for such a generous & patriotic offer & to inform you that I have communicated with the Medical Authorities, with a view to ascertaining their opinion as

to the most practical use
that could be made of these
horses & will inform you when
I hear from them. I regard
your offer of £200 per month,
for six months for the purpose
of obtaining all comforts, as a
most generous one & thank
you heartily for it.

Yrs truly,

Fred Montenik Wallem [illegible]
& party

To.
J. D. Logan Esq.
Tweeside Lodge,
Matjesfontein.

Waterloo Hotel
Edinburgh

Friday Morning
6. am
September 27th 1895

My own darling wife!

I have got up early this morning so as to be able to write you before the mail leaves and while I sit writing Jimmie is lying in bed beside the table fast asleep. He and myself left Reston on Wednesday morning for Dundee returning to Glasgow the same evening where we stayed at the Central Hotel where Mr. Broadbent and Mr. Sinclair met us and spent the evening, yesterday morning we started for a place below Paisley to see some Cartridges manufactured and returned to Glasgow again at midday We left there for Polmont about three oclock and spent an hour or two with Mr. Gray. he talks very highly of Jimmie and gives him a splendid character and says that throughout he has been a very good boy and never has any illness. The school commences on Tuesday so I will take him to the school myself and see that he is all right. As soon

going out. shopping as there
are a lot of things that the
wee chap requires. I only
wish I could get someone
else to do it as I hate shopping
Finlayson is away staying
with his sister just now so
I have a good chance of
getting through with my work.
My dearest Tibbie this is the
last letter but one that I
will write you as I hope
if God spares me to be with
you within a fortnight
after you receive this letter
I have fully decided to come
by the Scot which ought to
arrive in Cape Town on the
Monday. be sure and
come to Cape Town to meet

very much to see you again!
I hope that everything will
be finished and in apple
pie order by the time I
return. but I am sure you
will all have done the
best you can. I am far
from feeling well yet and
am getting very thin. but
still I am pleased to say
I am much better than I
was. I wont say any more
this mail as I hope to see you
soon now and give you all
the news so Good Bye for
this week and with all my
best love and kisses I
remain My dearest Tibbie
Your ever loving
Daddie

+ + + + + + +

CIVIL SERVICE CLUB,
CAPE TOWN.

5th Dec. 1895

My dear Jamie.

I've just wired you. "Think all right – Meanwhile impress on Elliott returning tonight (the) admirable manner you can work both provided (always your) tender (is the) highest" –

Elliott is expected back tomorrow morning and the final decision is delayed pending his return. The greatest

a very glowing report amending of "This is a most valuable mineral water". There's a meeting this aftn. to elect a committee of management. I proposed Johnson, Graaff & Pierson. My wife and I have given our patronage to an entertainment of Miss Fortescue's on Tuesday night. So I am sure to be in town next Tuesday & Wednesday in case you are coming up. Keep quiet for the present re the ADF. till you hear from them officially. Yr ever Dunning.

Secrecy is being maintained and no information is being vouchsafed to any one. – But you are going to get it: It's a very close run but you win by the shortest of short heads.

Don't forget my advice to feel your way very gently and meet the Railway Officials as far as you can: disabuse their minds of the fear or idea that you mean to try and run them, taking care of course all the same to protect your own interests.

They've mixed up the message to Lord Hawke at least I think so because he cabled to me asking "What team I propose getting up." I have not replied to London but telegraphed to Lord Hawke on board the Moor. Madeira that Logan (your name must have I'm inclined to think dropt out) has arranged everything most satisfactorily & will meet them on arrival. –

Dr. Haley has analysed the water of Days and gives

Telegraphic Address "Loganda" Cape Town.
P.O. Box 73 Cape Town

HEAD OFFICE:
Matjesfontein.
COUNTING HOUSE,
WAREHOUSES & BONDED STORES:
8 Adderley St Cape Town.
Branches throughout the
CAPE COLONY.
ORANGE FREE STATE.
GRIQUALAND WEST.
BECHUANALAND.
& RHODESIA.

James D. Logan & Co. Ltd.
Importers, Exporters & General Merchants
Refreshment & Advertising Contractors.
Matjesfontein. C.C.

Orange River

Tuesday Nov 21st 1899

My dear old wife /

We arrived here all right yesterday afternoon nothing the worse for our journey but the weather was awfully hot — I travelled part of the way with General French, who seemed a very nice man, and who will I think do good work in this part of the world — General Wauchope to whom I introduced you at Matjesfontein travelled in my company from De Aar and had an apology for a Luncheon with me, he is a very nice man although he could not assist me in any way in getting to the front —

The main body of our forces here amounting to some seven or eight thousand men left at day break today but of course can only go some eight miles from here before tonight.. but I learn that the Boers are in force about eight miles further on so that in all proba

...graphic Address: "Loganda. Cape Town."
...P.O. Box 78. Cape Town.

HEAD OFFICE:
Matjesfontein.
COUNTING HOUSE,
...EHOUSES & BONDED STORES:
...derley St. Cape Town.
...anches throughout the
CAPE COLONY,
ORANGE FREE STATE,
GRIQUALAND WEST,
BECHUANALAND,
& RHODESIA.

James D. Logan & Co. Ltd.
Importers, Exporters & General Merchants.
Refreshment & Advertising Contractors.
Matjesfontein, C.C.

will have a fight tomorrow. I have got very good horse and intend starting tomorrow at daylight when I hope to see some fun, but if there is no fighting nor any chance of getting to Kimberley before Friday I will come home on that day as promised.

A train went on this morning which will go about six miles from here. Penfold went with it. I think it is the best place for him. The officers all along the line laughed so much at that cap of his and made such fun at him that he was obliged to take it off. I tried so hard to chuck it out of the window only I had no opportunity of doing so. I hope to pass Penfold tomorrow morning about seven o'clock and join the main column about an hour later. The heat here is simply awful and the comforts anything but great consequently. I shall not be sorry when this wretched business is all over.

Telegraphic Address "Loganda" Cape Town
P.O. Box 73 Cape Town

HEAD OFFICE
Matjesfontein
COUNTING HOUSE,
WAREHOUSES & BONDED STORES
6 Adderley St. Cape Town
Branches throughout the
CAPE COLONY,
ORANGE FREE STATE.
GRIQUALAND WEST.
BECHUANALAND,
& RHODESIA.

James D. Logan & Co. Ltd.
Importers, Exporters & General Merchants.
Refreshment & Advertising Contractors.
Matjesfontein, C.C.

We have been and are very busy our takings for the last week being over three hundred pounds per day here. but now the troops have gone we will not be so busy for a bit.

Now my Bee & old Pet I think I have been very good in writing you such a long letter. and I hope if possible to be with you on Sunday. I have also written to Jimmie & Gertie today.

Good Bye for the present my dearest wife and with all the best of love. I am still

Your Ever Loving
Daddie

Good Bye God bless you
JDL

APPENDIX IV

DAVID RAWDON

RAWDON ON RAWDON – AN AUTOBIOGRAPHICAL NOTE

I came back from the Air Force in 1945. I had been a Rear Gunner in 31 Squadron and then in 604 RAF which was a Pathfinder Squadron and I had no idea what I wanted to do next. I had saved three-quarters of my monthly pay while in the airforce, which I used to buy a car. My father paid me five pounds a month for looking after our 20-acre place at Everton near Gillits and my mother let me have the banana and custard apple crops, which I was able to sell. I was in clover and could afford to go to Durban once a week to watch rugby and have a party. But after a while my parents began to worry that I lacked ambition and seemed settled for life. None of their suggestions for a career appealed to me. Eventually my father suggested that we buy a small hotel at Nottingham Road to serve the Michaelhouse parents. During the war my parents frequently had soldiers and sailors to stay. My mother noticed that nearly all troops drank a quart of beer at lunch and another before dinner and it seemed likely that this could be a profitable venture. We had all been to Hilton and seen how well the Hilton Hotel was doing. My father and I travelled up to Nottingham Road many times looking for a suitable site for an hotel on the main road without success. So regretfully we gave up the idea. He offered to send me to a famous hotel school in Lausanne, Switzerland.

I was not really keen on the idea, but my brother Graham said that if I did not want to go he would. So it was arranged for him to go to Europe for the four-year course.

I had always been crazy about horses. From the age of twelve I had always had a horse. So my father suggested I look for a job on a horse-breeding farm. This appealed to me and I managed to get a job on a month's trial with Labistour & Reynolds at Nottingham Road at eight pounds a month. After a month they invited me to stay on. Nine months later Joan Young asked me if I would like to go into partnership with her and her husband Reg to run a mobile store which would visit all the local farms.

My father was an American who came from a very poor family, all of whom had worked their way through university. He had qualified as a teacher initially and then went on to become a dentist. His two older brothers qualified as lawyers and became well known during the Prohibition period.

My father felt that this had done them no harm at all and had decided to give us each four hundred pounds towards a university education. I asked him if I could have my four hundred pounds to use as a deposit for the mobile store. He realised that I was not interested in going to university and he agreed.

Molly Reynolds heard about this and suggested that I invest the money in Reynolds shares, which had just been issued. Fortunately as a result my four hundred pounds became eight hundred.

We bought an old army dental van which I took up to Doves in Johannesburg. The husband of one of the Young girls whom I knew was a director, so for three weeks I worked under the supervision of the mortuary mechanic at Braamfontein, respraying the truck. I have many stories about my time there.

So we started the mobile store. I did all the driving. I was about twenty-three at the time. Three months later Joan and Reg's marriage broke up. She decided that she would like to take up his share of the partnership but as I was doing all the work at this stage, I agreed on condition she did half the driving. This proved to be too much for her so I bought them both out. I carried on running the store for four years during which time I built myself a house at Nottingham Road called Hawker's Cottage.

My mother's gardener, Ephraim, was my age and had worked for us since he was 13. He joined me and together we planted the gardens at Nottingham Road. He still works at the Nottingham Road Hotel, though he is semi-retired now. These days he only does the banking and the collecting of the post. We like to think of him as another Rawdon.

At this time my father sold our family property to Alec Blaikie for the amazing price of thirty thousand pounds. He had bought it for only two thousand pounds, but he had developed it and had made a beautiful garden there. By this time Graham had almost finished his four-year course in Lausanne. It so happened that the 50 acres of ground where the Nottingham Road Hotel now stands came up for sale at fifty pounds per acre. We decided to make a bid for it. It was absolutely bare open veld.

My father was willing to help us, but he said he would make the investment only if Graham and I went into it together. He could not do it for one of us only. We agreed and he lent us twenty thousand pounds and formed a company called G. Rawdon & Sons (Pty) Limited.

Graham got odd jobs and I was given the task of building the hotel with the assistance of a highly-skilled carpenter and local labour. We were up to window height when my father died suddenly of a heart attack. All my mother's friends tried to persuade her to stop the "folly" of the proposed hotel, but she said that it was her husband's dream and that she would honour his wishes and continue with the hotel.

It took us two years to build the hotel, which we opened in 1954. It was a great success, establishing me in my career as an hotelier and interior decorator, a career which I have found satisfying, fulfilling and profitable, and which has justified my parents' faith in me!

DAVID RAWDON - PROFESSIONAL CHRONOLOGY

Built hotel at Nottingham Road. Opened in 1954.

Bought Lanzerac 1958. Opened on 26th August 1959. Sold on ist August 1988.

Bought Matjiesfontein Village 1968. Opened on 1st November 1970.

Bought the Marine Hotel in October 1980. Re-opened on the 20th December 1985.

Engaged to decorate the Drostdy Hotel, Graaf-Reinet, which was restored by Historical Homes S.A. Limited. Opened in October 1977 and ran it on a management basis during 1978 / 1979.

Engaged to re-decorate part of the Durban Club in November 1977.

Engaged to re-decorate part of Spinney Green, Olifantsfontein 1979.

Engaged to re-decorate part of Kelvin Grove Club in 1980.

Engaged to re-decorate Rembrandt's Court House in Johannesburg in 1980.

Engaged to re-decorate Fleur du Cap in 1981.

Earlier commissions:

Amanzimnyama, Tongaat Group 'Pie"ddquarters at Tongaat.

Fleur du Cap for the Rembrandt Group.

Matjiesfontein

APPENDIX V

MATJIESFONTEIN REVISITED

The Laird's Arms

"The Laird's Arms", adjoining the hotel, is very reminiscent of an English pub. However, this building was initially used as a carpenter's shop by two Scottish carpenters who had been brought out by Logan from Scotland to do all the carpentry for the village. Later it became a butcher's shop. Then, during World War II Jimmy Logan and his sister Gertrude and her husband turned it into a recreation room for R.N. sailors on leave at Simonstown. After the war it served for some years as the Village Hall.

Matjiesfontein Museum

This museum was originally housed in one of the small cottages in the main street. However, with the countrywide decline in rail traffic and the advent of computers, many of the smaller railway stations were virtually closed down. This sad fate also overtook the station at Matjiesfontein, the beautiful station building no longer being thought of as necessary. The railway authorities accordingly turned two rooms of the building into a railway museum which is well worth a visit.

The rest of the extensive building, including the cellars which run underneath it, was leased to David Rawdon. One room became a conference room while the remainder of the building was converted to house the Matjiesfontein Museum.

An exhibit of great interest is a large camera display with an extensive collection of cameras, dating from way back to the present day.

The museum offers an olden-day apothecary's shop and barber's shop and in addition, the cellars boast a superb collection of Victorian china, glass, dolls and furniture.

A number of military exhibits grace the museum, including soldiers' uniforms and guns and the odd more unusual item, such as a campaign toilet chest that would accompany high-ranking officers on campaign. Firemen's clothing and firemen's helmets also form part of the display.

One exhibit tells an interesting story. It is an original 'Logan' soup plate acquired nearly a century ago by a small boy travelling with his parents by rail and stopping at Matjesfontein for refreshments.

When the train whistle blew, signalling the imminent departure of the train, this small boy determined not to be deprived of his hot soup, boarded the train soup plate in hand, much to the embarrassment of his family!

This soup plate remained for many years a prized heirloom, until a family member recently decided that it belonged more properly in the Matjiesfontein Museum and duly returned it to David Rawdon complete with this charming story.

Another prime exhibit is Jimmy Logan junior's impressive collection of animal heads.

This delightful museum even hosts, rather incongruously for a venue so far from the sea, a large collection of ship's lights and lanterns!

The Lord Milner Hotel

Nowhere is the magic of Matjiesfontein more tangible than in the Lord Milner Hotel itself. Just one step into the brick - paved courtyard with its enchanting fountain and wrought iron chairs and tables is enough to take one back in time. Beyond the ornate doors leading into the courtyard from the hotel lies a veritable treasure house of antique furniture, pictures and other objet d'art, most of it dating from Victorian times.

The design of the Hotel and its furnishings are as follows (as reproduced from the brochure on the Lord Milner Hotel printed for the Matjiesfontein centenary of 1984):

The Lord Milner Hotel

at

MATJIESFONTEIN

in the

REPUBLIC OF SOUTH AFRICA

NOTES ON THE FURNISHING OF
THE RECEPTION ROOMS

1884 100 MATJIESFONTEIN 1984

INTRODUCTION

The hotel was built just before the outbreak of the Anglo-Boer War, and named the Milner Hotel after Sir Alfred Milner, then the Governor of the Cape Colony. The structure of the building has remained unaltered, and certain of the fixtures and furniture are also original, for example the dining room buffet tables, and the main staircase.

However most of the furniture and furnishings were brought here later in the 1960's when the hotel was revived under the direction of Mr David Rawdon, and reopened in 1970 as The Lord Milner Hotel. Since then it has become renowned for its comfort, fine cuisine, good service, and not least its decor, which places well-chosen antiques in an authentic late-nineteenth century setting.

Notes on the history of Matjiesfontein are available in a separate leaflet, but are also included at the back of this booklet for convenience.

CAPTAIN S BANKS, RN FRSA
Vice Chairman,
Antique Collectors' Society
of South Africa

VOORWOORD

Die Milner Hotel is kort voor die uitbreek van die Anglo-Boere Oorlog gebou en is vernoem na Sir Alfred Milner, die destydse Goewerneur van die Kaap Kolonie. Die boustruktuur van die gebou het onveranderd gebly en sekere vaste toebehore en meubelstukke is ook oorspronklik soos byvoorbeeld die hooftrap en buffettafels in die eetkamer.

Die grootste deel van die meubels is egter in die laat sestigerjare hierheen gebring toe die hotel onder die aanwysing van mnr David Rawdon gerestoureer is en in 1970 as die Lord Milner Hotel heropen is. Sederdien het dit bekendheid verwerf vir gemak, heerlike etes, goeie diens en veral die decor, wat welgekose antieke stukke in 'n outentieke laat-neentiende eeuse agtergrond plaas.

Notas aangaande die geskiedenis van Matjiesfontein is beskikbaar in 'n aparte blaadjie, maar is ook geriefshalwe agter in hierdie boekie ingesluit.

KAPT. S. BANKS, RN FRSA
Vise-voorsitter,
Outhede Versamelaars Vereniging
va Suid-Afrika

THE CROWN PRINCE AND PRINCESS OF PRUSSIA
IN ABOUT THE YEAR 1870

HALL

1. The marble busts on either side of the front door are of the Crown Prince and Princess of Prussia. She was the eldest daughter of Queen Victoria. They were married in 1858. He became Kaiser Frederick III in 1888 but died the same year, and was succeeded by their son as Kaiser Wilhelm II, who eventually died in exile in 1941. These busts came from the German Club in Port Elizabeth.

2. Gros point embroidery by Agnes Nimmo, worked in 1879. Full details are given on a brass plate at the bottom of the frame.

3. Oil painting of an unkown lady, dressed in the fashion of about 1900.

4. A pair of marble busts of children, in the style of ancient Rome, but Italian 19th century.

5. Glazed terracotta plaques of Ganymede on his eagle, and cherubs forging the thunderbolts of Jove. Early 20th century studio work, perhaps Florentine.

6. The subject of this fine portrait of a seated gentleman is not known, nor is the painter, although there is a signature and the date 1916 at the top on the right. It is thought that the sitter may have been one of the Johannesburg pioneers.

7. On the under sides of the upper flights of stairs are 'Grecian maenad' figures in papier maché. They date from the building of the hotel in the last years of the 19th century.

8. A mid-19th century desk veneered in flame mahogany. The chairs on either side were made in the short reign of William IV, just before that of Queen Victoria.

9. A late 19th century mercury barometer in Gothic style. The banjo-shaped aneroid barometer was already more usual when this one was made.

* * * * * *

DINING ROOM

10. The lacquered cast iron pillar which holds up the ceiling is a splendid example of late 19th century ironfounding. Although slim and elegant, it supports a considerable weight.

11. The floor covering is of 'Elephant Quality' linoleum and, believe it or not, has lain here for over eighty years.

12. This 19th century clock is a typical presentation piece of its period, heavy and ornate. Bracket clocks such as this, but much lighter in weight, were made in earlier centuries to be carried from room to room as the only clock in a house.

13. These prints of tropical fruits and flowers, here and also in the long corridor upstairs (see No. 58) are chromolithographs by Mme. Berthe van Nooten, painted by her in Batavia, and published in Brussels about 1870. The one second on the right from the entrance door shows a 'finger citron'. This was carved in jade by the Chinese, when it came to be called a 'Buddha's hand'.

HALL AND DINING ROOM

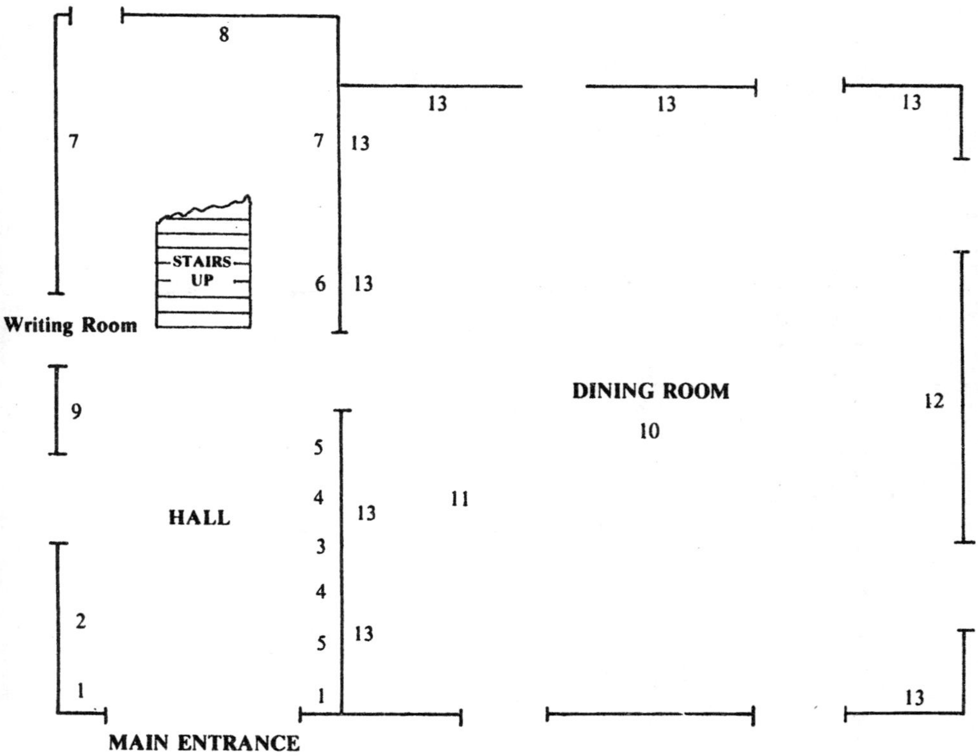

SITTING ROOMS

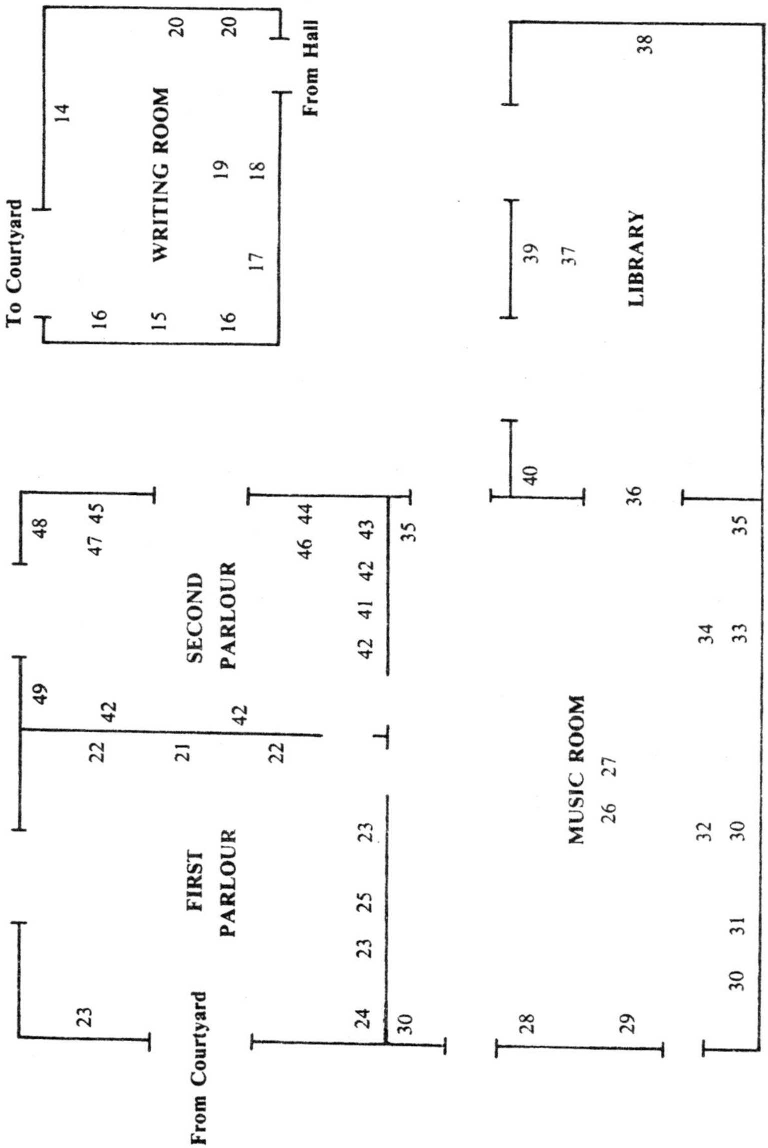

WRITING ROOM

14. A Staffordshire pottery mid-19th century figure group, moulded on the base 'Prince and Princess'. This is the Princess Royal and the Crown Prince of Prussia, soon after their engagement in 1855. See No. 1 for this couple in later years.

15. A late 18th century bureau bookcase. Note the Gothic arcading which supports the glass, the small drawers faced with satinwood, and the stamped brass handles to the large drawers. The feet of this piece have been renewed, but it is otherwise in original condition.

16. A pair of Berlin woolwork Biblical scenes in original frames. It was in the 1820's that a printer in Berlin first sold squares of canvas printed in outlines, and hanks of the necessary coloured wools to embroider them. The idea caught on, and remained a hobby of leisured women until the end of the century.

17. This is something a little better; a raised woolwork picture of a King Charles spanial, probably the owner's pet in about 1850.

18. Here is a pole screen, to protect delicate complexions from the heat of the parlour fire. It is filled with Berlin woolwork of about 1860, showing that devoted old couple Darby and Joan, who first appeared in a ballad a good hundred years before.

19. On the mantelpiece is a box of 'Pontypool' ware. About 1730 an ironmaster of that South Wales town invented a lacquer derived from coal tar which when applied to sheet iron preserved it from heat and rust and gave it a pleasant shiny brown look. This box was made about 1830 to store tea or other groceries.

20. A pair of prints after paintings by Francis Wheatley. This artist portrayed working class people sympathetically, which was unusual in the 18th century. There are many interesting details in these prints.

Leave the Writing Room by its outside door, and walk along the side of the courtyard to the last door on the right leading into the First Parlour.

* * * * * *

FIRST PARLOUR

21. Round the low table is a suite of two chairs and a settee. These were for a modest parlour in the middle of last century; a chair each for the master and mistress, and a settee for two visitors. The original upholstery would have been deep, and buttoned.

22. On either side of the settee are early 19th century dining chairs, with sabre legs and rope-cut back rails. These are nowadays called Trafalgar chairs, because of the rope-cut rails, one may suppose.

23. Embroidery was a necessary female accomplishment, and every girl had to prove her ability by working a sampler. Notice on the right of the courtyard door a sampler showing a map of England which gives the names of only Yorkshire towns, including Scarborough, a small seaside resort. It is not difficult to guess that the young needlewoman came from there.

24. A xylophone in an Edwardian wood frame. Each bar of the instrument has a brass sound-box. This xylophone is still used on occasions to summon the hotel guests.

25. An early 20th century silver-plated tantalus, complete with key. It would be 'tantalising' to see the spirits in the decanters but not to be able to pour them out.

MUSIC ROOM

26. A 'square' Broadwood piano of about 1850, with a metal frame. This is a late example of its kind, made when most pianos were either 'upright' or 'grand', though the square piano remained popular in the USA until the 1880's.

27. A fine gilt metal and glass chandelier, converted to electricity. The vine with abundant clusters of grapes gives a date for it in the 1850's, the 'high Victorian' period. This chandelier was bought at the Sir Abe Bailey sale.

28. A black japanned and painted coal scuttle of late 19th century date. Note that it is mounted on wheels!

29. This is a Sanctus bell, made to be sounded in church at solemn moments in the service of the Mass.

30. These coloured mezzotints of cherubs playing are from pictures by Lady Diana Beauclerk (1734 – 1808), a talented amateur painter. They were published in London in 1801, and are in their original frames.

31. This is a Georgian 'night table' or 'bedside commode'. The deep drawer contained a chamber pot.

32. An early 19th century harp from the London firm of Sébastian Érard (1752 – 1831), the foremost maker of his time. In 1808 he patented a system of pedals which allowed changes of key. Erard was French, but had a factory in London from the outbreak of the French Revolution, in 1792.

33. A plain and useful chest of drawers, veneered in mahogany, made about 1750. Note that the drawers are graduated in depth from top to bottom.

34. A copper samovar for boiling tea water, possibly Turkish. The kettle and its brazier are now soldered together and the contraption converted to electricity.

35. Two tub chairs of Edwardian date, decorated in lacquer. Small and light, this sort of furniture is now popular.

* * * * * *

LIBRARY

36. The leather panelled entrance doors are from a bar room in the Mount Nelson Hotel in Cape Town.

37. An oak tip-up table from the middle of the 18th century. Although mahogany was then fashionable, much plain oak furniture such as this continued to be made.

38. A gilt wood and gesso overmantel in 'Chinese Chippendale' style, but this is a 19th century piece. The pottery figure of a sage on a bracket at the top was probably supplied with the mirror.

39. Plaster death mask of a young girl whose drowned body was found in the Seine. The peaceful expression on her face still exerts its charm.

40. An early 20th century side table with a parquetry top, in the style of the late 17th century.

SECOND PARLOUR

41. A writing desk of pine veneered with sycamore. This is an unusual piece of furniture, in 'biedermeier' style, made about 1840 in Germany, or Austria

42. Four pictures on glass of frigates, in their traditional maplewood frames with gilt insets.

43. A wine table of mahogany. Tables such as this were used by our ancestors, who sat upright in their chairs. When in the middle of last century the easy chair came in, the wine table went out. This particular one is a modern reproduction.

44. Steel engraving of HRH The Duke of York after a painting by Sir Thomas Lawrence. The frame, and that of No. 45 below, is original. The Queen's Crown at the top suggests that both were framed to hang in some royal residence after Queen Victoria came to the throne.

45. Lithograph of King George IV dated 1824, that is three years after his accession.

46. Staffordshire pottery figure of Queen Victoria as a young matron. The almost obliterated inscription on the base refers to her as Empress of India, and reads 'Year of Jubilee', so the figure must have been issued, or more probably reissued, after 1876.

47. Staffordshire pottery figure of The Prince of Wales, later Edward VII. It shows him as a man about thirty years old, dating the figure to about 1870.

48. Amateur watercolour portrait of a young man wearing the round jacket of a naval midshipman. It is marked on the back 'Jack Hathorn, born 1800, died 1839'. We are not told how his short life was ended.

49. A 'grandfather' clock from Yorkshire with a painted dial, such as was to be found in the houses of small farmers and artisans in about 1840. The movement runs for thirty hours, so needs to be wound daily: more expensive clocks ran for eight days, so only required attention once a week.

* * * * * *

UPSTAIRS

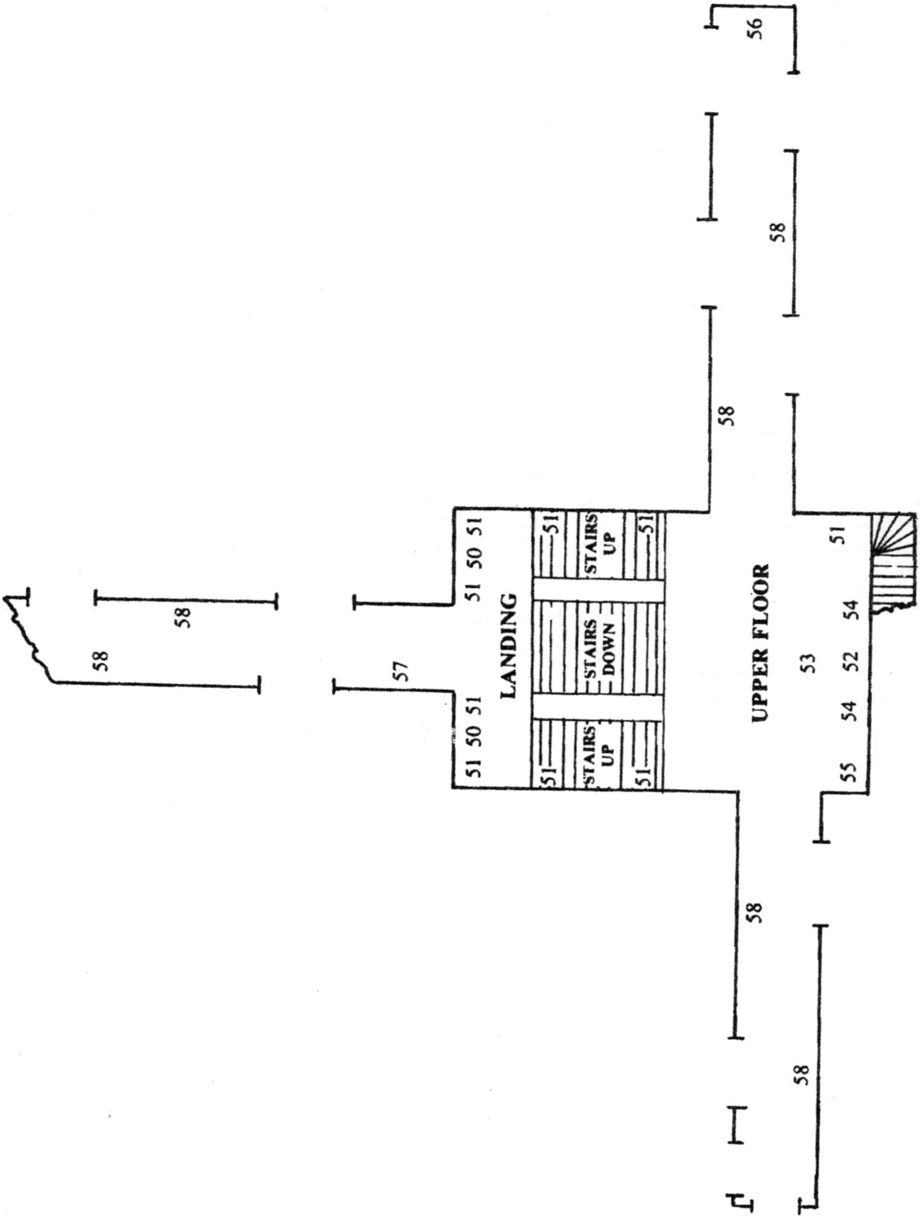

LANDING
UPPER FLOOR
STAIRS UP
STAIRS DOWN
STAIRS UP
51
50
52
53
54
55
56
57
58

PLEASE NOTE:
IT IS REGRETTED THAT ONLY RESIDENTS IN THE HOTEL ARE ALLOWED UPSTAIRS

STAIRWELL AND FIRST FLOOR CORRIDORS

50. Late 19th century cast iron brackets for oil lamps, converted to electricity.

51. Pictures on glass of 19th century soldiers, three of them from the book ‘Officers of the British Army’.

52. A mule chest of oak dated 1752. The ‘mule chest’, so called because it was a cross between a medieval chest (‘kist’) and a chest of drawers, was first made in the late 17th century.

53. A candelabra in Anglo-Egyptian style, probably from an Army officers’ mess, late 19th century.

54. A pair of Staffordshire pottery spaniel dogs, late 19th century. These were known as ‘comforters’, because their soulful expressions gave solace to lonely people in their homes.

55. An early Victorian pole screen with beadwork filling. See also No. 18.

56. A plaster bust of a girl, published by Friedring Goldscherde in Vienna about 1910. It is in the Austrian ‘Secession’ style.

57. A marble bust of a boy depicting Winter, no doubt one of a pair with a girl depicting Summer. French, 19th century.

58. Flower and fruit prints, as described under No. 13. The one at the extreme end on the right is of Tradescantia, often seen these days as a pot plant.